Confessions
of a
Learner
Parent

Parenting like a boss.
(An inexperienced, slightly ineffectual boss.)

Sam Avery

SEVEN DIALS

First published in Great Britain in 2017
by Seven Dials
An imprint of Orion Publishing Group Ltd
Carmelite House, 50 Victoria Embankment, London, EC4Y 0DZ

An Hachette UK Company

5 7 9 10 8 6 4

Text © Sam Avery 2017

A CIP catalogue record for this book
is available from the British Library.

Hardback ISBN: 9781409175636
Ebook ISBN: 9781409175643

Cover illustration: Jessie Ford

Printed and bound in Great Britain by
Clays Ltd, Elcograf S.p.A.

www.orionbooks.co.uk

For Ben, Zac and Rachel,
without whom my life, and these pages, would be blank.

Contents

Diary of a Two-Year-Old (whose Dad is maybe writing a book)

MONDAY

Daddy seems to be watching me more intently at the moment. Feels like he's willing me to do something idiotic and when I do, he laughs to himself and writes in a notebook. Weird. Maybe he's writing a book. I hope Peppa Pig's in it.

TUESDAY

Had SIX absolute meltdowns today. Two at breakfast, three at lunch and two in the car. Is that seven? Okay, I had SEVEN absolute meltdowns today. Oh and one just before bedtime. So, eight - EIGHT meltdowns. And one in the bath. Crap, that's nine isn't it? Or ten if you count when someone stole my crayon in playgroup and I cried so hard I nearly swallowed my own head. Tell you what, let's call it fifteen to be on the safe side - I had FIFTEEN massive, all-out meltdowns today.

Other than that I was on top form.

WEDNESDAY

Refused to take my nap today - was convinced something amazing was going to happen and didn't want to miss it. Nothing happened. Got annoyed.

THURSDAY

Went to this amazing theme park today called IKEA and it was brilliant even though all of the Big People looked really miserable the whole time. I don't understand - why would you CHOOSE to do something that makes you sad? That'd be like me turning the telly off or sharing. I loved it though - tonnes of hazards to trip over, loads of stuff to grab and a big mad trolley with no baby seats so they couldn't strap me down. I went bananas, running about worse than Daddy that time when he was asleep on the sofa and I jumped on his goolies. At one point there were about a million beds to climb on and I didn't want to go home but they said we had to so they tried saying they were leaving without me, thinking I'd cave and run towards them, but I was over the bloody moon. That place is well better than our house.

FRIDAY

Spoke to Nana today. Sometimes I can't believe she lives inside that iPad.

SATURDAY

Did a synchronised nappy leak with my brother today. We've been trying to time this for ages but he always goes too early which leaves me squeezing and straining while he wanders off to stink out a different room. Today we made eye contact and counted to three before unleashing total hell and giggling our little heads off. Doubt we'll ever go back to John Lewis with Mummy again.

SUNDAY

Spilled juice all over Daddy's laptop. He started flapping like a big hairy bird shouting 'MY BOOK! OH GOD! MY BOOK!' so I gave him the Peppa Pig one I was reading to compensate. He didn't seem interested, which I thought was pretty rude to be honest. I'll never understand Big People.

Sam Says 'Hello'

I'm writing this at four o'clock on a Sunday morning. A decade ago, this time of the week would have seen me holding a kebab whilst fabulously drunk after an almighty night out at The Krazyhouse (our local rock club). It's a similar picture today, if by drunk you mean 'exhausted' and by kebab you mean 'small child'. There's other similarities with 10 years ago too – I'm barely conscious, slurring my words and there's a strong chance I'll end up with puke on my trousers – although these days it's not from necking vodka Red Bulls but instead because I'm a dad to toddler twins. (If you have kids yourself then this will all make perfect sense. If you don't have kids then you're a brave soul for picking up this book and I salute you. These confessions are not for the faint-hearted.)

Becoming a parent is the most beautiful trauma I have ever experienced. It's also not what I expected. When kids arrive your life becomes full of tiny contradictions. Your home fills up with more love than you thought humanly possible while simultaneously stinking like a tramp's duffel coat pocket. You gain a renewed sense of purpose and feel unspeakable joy, yet some days you can't remember either as exhaustion has caused you to leave the house wearing slippers on the wrong feet. The magical times might make everything else worthwhile but it's hard to recall your baby's first smile when you're scraping dried porridge off the kitchen wall with a razor blade.

When my kids were born people told me to 'enjoy every single moment'. Now, that's just not realistic when you feel like a malnourished zombie who'd do time for a lie-in. Sleep deprivation makes everything difficult. It's an all-consuming soup of confusion that descends and takes charge like a dozy supply teacher. I was once so burnt-out I spent five minutes queuing up behind a row of parked cars.

But I didn't want to forget the good bits, because, in amongst the exploding nappies and the teething trauma and the time my son shut down a swimming pool with his floaters, there was so much magic. So I started writing it down, and this turned into a blog. I called myself 'The Learner Parent', because parenting is all about learning, isn't it? Normally by fucking things up first.

I've learned so much since becoming a parent – lessons about myself and my kids, and about which things in life truly have meaning. My training has been slow and sometimes painful, especially the practical elements. I've struggled with nappies, bottles and prams, usually getting them down pat just before my kids move on to the next phase, rendering my new-found skills utterly redundant. Who knew that being able to dead-lift a 30lb shitting toddler over an unsteady baby gate while trying to remember the exact order of verses for 'The Wheels on the Bus' would be part of my basic training?

I wanted to write this book because I've been fortunate to witness, through my blog, the positive impact of funny, honest stories about those days when we fall somewhat short of parenting perfection. They seem to puncture through the loneliness and connect us into one big parent gaggle. And they can encourage us to admit when we're struggling. Because we all struggle.

I'm lucky to have a lively and vocal following on my Facebook page, and over the years I've filed the feedback I get into three categories:

1. Parents thanking me that someone has been so honest about their own failings.
2. New mums and dads who've had a tough day but say my latest post has cheered them up.
3. People who tell me that the blog has completely put them off having kids. (Someone even suggested that I should give talks in schools to reduce teenage pregnancy. Ha!)

But enough about me. In fact, let me introduce you to some of the people you'll meet in this book.

Rachel: The Wife

I love my wife for a million reasons. She's kind, loving, supportive and patient. She's the funniest person I've ever met and makes me laugh every day, mainly at my own expense. We first met at a stand-up gig I was doing and she's been heckling me ever since.

Zac and Ben: The Kids

Our identical twin boys. They shared a womb for eight months but now won't even share a drink. They're funny, kind and, if the wind's blowing the wrong way, a bloody nightmare. They have changed my life in immeasurable ways and have most likely taken value off the house with some of the bodily fluids they've ejected.

June and Dave AKA Mum and Dad: My Parents

One of my early lessons as a new dad was to realise how ungrateful I had been to my own parents while growing up. I'd like to take this as an opportunity to say a huge sorry to my mum and dad. They did nothing but work tirelessly to give my younger brother and me a good start in life and in return, we acted like a pair of odious little turds. Every time my sons are uncooperative or wiping snot on the furniture I get a tiny bit closer to understanding what my parents went through with us.

For a time, my mum and dad worried they'd never get the chance to be grandparents and I politely remind them of this every time I need them to babysit at the last minute.

Janet: Rachel's Mum

I'm a stand-up comedian and she's my mother-in-law so from a comedic point of view this should have been a match made in heaven. Rather selfishly, Janet chose not to fit any of the stereotypical mother-in-law characteristics and instead has been supportive, helpful and a fantastic grandparent to the boys. Where's the comedy in that?

Now you've met all of the main characters, what better place to start than the beginning? I'm going to share with you everything I've learned (so far) on this crazy parent journey from my own point of view – a new dad in his 30s with the sense of humour of someone half his age.

Part 1:

The Road to Parenthood

The Trying Game

I always wanted kids, but then again, I've always wanted a loft conversion. Both are pretty easy to put off as they're very expensive and tend to wreck your house. My wife and I had just tied the knot and were basking in the nuptial afterglow on our honeymoon. We'd saved up for years to afford a once-in-a-lifetime trip to Barbados. Five-star hotel, all-inclusive. We had just come down to breakfast and were sitting in the morning sun as the Atlantic Ocean lapped against the golden shore.

I didn't have a care in the world.

Rachel took her sunglasses off and put them on the table. 'We should start trying soon.'

'Yeah, I already know what I want so I'll grab the waiter next time he walks past,' I said, innocently looking around for the man who'd shown us to our table.

'Not the food. We should start, you know, *trying*.'

Trying?

I glanced down at my sunburnt midriff. I thought I *was* trying. I'd had a shave that morning and was wearing a brand-new Hawaiian shirt from Matalan. Anyway, we were married now, and there's a strong argument that after the pre-wedding healthy-eating regime the honeymoon is the exact moment when you can *stop* trying.

A lady walked past our table carrying a baby. Rachel's eyes followed them. The penny dropped.

She meant *trying*. She was talking about kids. *Bloody hell*, I thought. *Already*?

The waiter interrupted our family-planning meeting and asked what we were having.

Resisting the urge to shout 'A BABY APPARENTLY!' I instead ordered the traditional Barbados breakfast: a full English with all the trimmings.

'How are you having your eggs, sir?'

It would have been easy to say 'fertilised' but I told him to surprise me, in keeping with the theme of the morning.

I don't know why it *was* a surprise. We'd talked about this lots of times and we both wanted kids. We'd also just got married, so, according to societal peer pressure, the next logical step was to think about children. But in my head, being newlyweds meant we were entitled to a two-year buffer zone before we even had to think about starting to try. Wasn't that the rule?

'Can't we at least enjoy being married for a while?' I offered.

I'd used a similar piss-poor excuse the day after our engagement when she came home with a stack of wedding magazines. My mind hadn't made the very natural connection between asking somebody to marry you and then actually marrying that somebody.

'You're 36, I'm 31. Even if we got pregnant this afternoon, you'd still be 40 by the time the baby started school.'

'This afternoon? I thought we had that boat trip booked?'

'I'm talking hypothetically. You don't want to be an old dad.'

She was right, I didn't. I've got nothing against old dads, but then I've got nothing against bin men – I just didn't want to be one. Mick Jagger's probably still going to be reproducing well into his 90s, but you get the distinct impression he's not getting up for the night feed or peeling dried sick off his leather trousers on the way to rehearsals.

We couldn't put this off indefinitely like you do when the kitchen needs re-grouting. We did need to start trying soon.

Bloody hell.

Our breakfast arrived and my eggs were scrambled, just like my head.

We didn't start trying immediately (there was the boat trip after all). I managed to persuade Rachel to wait an entire month, having made the case that there was a lot of other stuff to get in order first. We were pretty broke after the wedding and the honeymoon, and there was some serious work needed on the house. The kitchen was a mess and the bathroom needed decorating. I'm also very fond of sleep and I quite like money, and despite never having much of either I knew that the arrival of a baby would make my quest to achieve an unlimited supply of both impossible.

Of course, these were just distractions from my real reason to delay everything: I wasn't *quite* ready. Both Rachel and I were in our thirties and we had a great relationship. We had reasonably steady incomes and a mortgage. Bar a few credit-card bills and two post graduate loans we were still chipping away at, we didn't have any massive debts. But it still didn't feel like the Perfect Time.

As much as I wanted to become a dad 'someday', I viewed parenthood with a certain level of suspicion. It looked like lots of fun, but then so was going out for dinner once a week, having absolutely no responsibilities and lying in bed till midday at weekends. I'd seen friends of mine become parents and age alarmingly – almost immediately, practically withering in front of my eyes like old vinyl LPs left out in the sun.

Some years earlier, we'd bumped into an old university friend of mine in the supermarket. Back in the day he'd been the ultimate party boy – always out on the tiles and the last man standing at the bar. Since I'd last seen him he'd had two kids, and as our trolleys converged in the middle of Asda I almost didn't recognise him.

'Sam?'

'Holy shit, IS THAT ALAN?!' (That's not his real name – party boys don't tend to be called Alan.)

I couldn't believe it. His skin was ghoulishly pale and his once-resplendent bouffant had all but disappeared. He hadn't aged particularly badly (he looked good for someone who was 40), just very quickly (he was only 26).

The Travolta-strut he once prowled the clubs and bars with had been replaced by a lethargic, confused shuffle as he pushed his screaming baby round the supermarket with all the elegance of someone on their way to an audition for *The Walking Dead*. Meanwhile, his toddler daughter had gone rogue and was ricocheting down the frozen-food aisle, slamming into freezers and ripping open boxes of waffles while shouting, 'LOOK AT THE SIZE OF THIS LEGO, DADDY!'

He requested that she stop her systematic destruction of the shop with that ineffective combination of high volume and zero conviction – a commonly used tactic deployed by most parents at some point.

What in the name of intergalactic buggery had happened to Mr Saturday Night?

Quite simply, he'd become a dad. And it appeared that the by-product of fathering two kids was that he'd lost all his standards and most of his hair. I felt fortunate not to have bumped into him outside, as chances are I would've mistaken him for a homeless person and tried to pop a 50-pence piece into his take-out Americano cup.

We made casual remarks about meeting up for a drink but I knew it wouldn't happen. Because that was the other side-effect of parenthood that didn't seem too enticing: all my friends who'd had kids dramatically disappeared from the social radar, as if they'd been taken down by a nappy-wearing sniper. Sometimes this wasn't even a bad thing either, as most of them had no conversation to bring to the table post-kids, other than stories about their children, parenting and 'how hard it all was'.

Yawn.

I NEVER wanted to be like that.

(Ladies and gentlemen, look at me now! A parent blogger who's also the proud author of this book about PARENTING. It's clear that the day my kids were born I didn't JUST become a father, I also became a hypocrite.)

So if you're anything like me, a pregnancy (whether still in discussion or already in the womb) will get you fretting and fidgeting like a pigeon with PTSD.

I started to worry about everything.

Top fear number 1: Would I be a good dad? Loads of friends had told me they thought I'd make a great dad but the subtext I got from this was: 'Sam, you're REALLY immature so your kids will be on the same wavelength.' I knew it would take more than a love of American wrestling and a keen sense of toilet humour to get me through this.

Top fear number 2: Could we cope financially? Despite regular work for both of us, some months our finances were tighter than Bono's trousers, so factoring in the purchase of all the baby essentials alongside Rachel's drop to statutory maternity pay seemed like economic suicide.

And top fear number 3: Was the world a safe enough place to bring more people into? What with climate change, trouble in the Middle East and the growing threat of a Westlife reunion, surely it wasn't humane to subject anyone to these potential horrors?

I understand now that the Perfect Time to fall pregnant doesn't actually exist, unless you happen to impregnate your partner whilst simultaneously taking a penny to a winning scratch card.

After all my misgivings and self-doubt, Rachel managed to convince me with a simple and effective counterargument.

'You know to conceive we'll have to have loads of sex.'

I hadn't thought of it like that.

Commence Project Baby

It's difficult to become a parent without some good old-fashioned sex. Not that our sex was particularly old-fashioned – there was never a Penny Farthing involved – but I can't really talk about parenthood without explaining how we got there. So dim the lights, stick that old Barry White album on repeat and put down your sandwich, because the next few chapters will contain what my dear old nan always referred to as 'relations'. Usually in a comically theatrical whisper that was actually *louder* than her speaking voice.

Don't worry though, it won't get too graphic. This isn't part of the *Fifty Shades* series. I'm also acutely aware that one day my kids might read this and I'm not keen on them knowing all of the *ins and outs*, if you'll pardon the expression. My wife also made the legitimate point that anything written about my sexual prowess would be very short indeed. So here goes.

We didn't tell anyone we'd begun to try and make a baby. I've always found it unsettling when friends announce during dinner that they've 'started trying', as it basically translates as 'We are currently shagging lots.' A surefire way to put you off your pavlova. A friend I bumped into once informed me that he and his missus had recently started 'trying *properly*', which suggested that previously they'd only been trying *improperly*. To me, that sounded like bottoms had been involved, which wasn't information I was hungry for in the middle of Debenhams.

Remember how Rachel persuaded me to have a baby with the shameless promise of unlimited sex? Well, it's amazing how you think that trying for a baby will just be months of red-hot, dirty pumping with your partner. Of course, the moment you start using phrases like 'red-hot, dirty pumping' then your partner will quite rightly refuse to come anywhere near you. Other slang terms subsequently banned from my vocabulary included 'rumpy-pumpy', 'slap and tickle' and 'rodgering'. (I've often wondered why the term 'rodgering' is used to describe sexual intercourse. The name Rodger isn't sexy in the slightest – even Alan is more likely to get the blood pumping. If your name is Rodger or Alan this is probably all quite offensive. I'll stop now.)

Sex should be something you do because the moment takes you – except on special occasions like anniversaries or birthdays, when it's normally planned in to the schedule (and is admittedly difficult if the kids have gone to bed and you're attempting a 'danger-bonk' on the bouncy castle). Romantically, it's two lovers (or three if you're greedy), losing yourselves in a passionate exchange that brings your minds and souls closer together. If it's early in the relation-ship you've probably just had a spontaneous quickie on the couch during the ad break for *Grand Designs*, and you'll lie in each other's arms, sweat glistening across half-naked bodies, gazing into your partner's eyes. Five years on, you're definitely still open to sex during the ad break, but now it's only so you don't miss any of your favourite programme. (And that buzzer noise during *Britain's Got Talent* would put you right off your stroke anyway.)

The second you start trying for a baby all spontaneity evaporates like steam from an outdoor piss. You and your partner become a corporation with clear aims, outputs and a mission statement. That just isn't sexy, no matter which font you choose to type up the minutes in.

My wife assumed the role of project manager, which I presumed made me chief executive. Before I could go all Christian Grey and explain how this had always been a particular fantasy of mine she was quick to point out that she was the boss. So I stuck the kettle on and we began the super-sexy task of diary coordinating. I don't know about you but nothing gets me more batshit horny than leafing through calendars and checking date clashes.

Phwooaar!

We both had busy schedules so we planned to begin our new project the following Friday night. The mission was a go.

The first lesson I learned about parenthood, way before I became an actual parent, was that there's something very different about sex with your partner the first time you're trying to conceive. It feels more grown-up, deliberate even (I know 'accidental sex' doesn't really exist, unless perhaps you're part of an unfortunate high-speed pile-up at the roller disco). Maybe you spend your Sundays posing as a life model or have recently had your prostate examined, but otherwise, baby-making sex is as serious as you can get without your pants on.

The previously sexy dirty talk changes quite dramatically too.

'I can't wait to get you home so I can carefully lay you on the bed for some unprotected, highly efficient, reproductive sexual intercourse.'

'Will you hold my legs in the air afterwards while I do bicycle kicks?'

'Course I will, you dirty bitch.'

As a typical man, I made the whole thing all about me. This wasn't a collaborative process between our reproductive systems – it was basically a job interview for my semen. And with my classic male ego, I was quietly convinced that I could seal the deal the first time out. To use a basketball analogy, the bucket was open and I just had to get to the scoring zone and slam-dunk the ball. Ideally with no dribbling. Then I undertook some light research and was concerned to read that a man's sexual peak is when he's just 18. That meant that when my libido was at the peak of its powers – the sexual equivalent of Guns N' Roses circa 1987 – literally nobody wanted to enjoy its rampant benefits. I was now 36 – nearly 20 years past my best – which meant my penis was more like an old gunslinger with a drink problem and low self-esteem, coming back for one last shoot-out. (Did you listen to Guns N' Roses' latest album? Utter tripe.) But, regardless of the sexual landscape, I was up for the challenge.

And then after just one 'steamy' session that, in Rachel's words, she 'could have timed a boiled egg to', her period was a day late! My sperm had clearly done the job already and was the testicular equivalent of Michael Jordan.

Nothing but net.

Before I could buy a box of cigars and a baby name book, she came on. Turns out my little swimmers were nothing special after all.

Relax. Don't Do It.
(But Keep Doing It.)

Maybe you're more clued-up than me, but I thought getting pregnant would be a piece of piss, like booking a holiday: you decide when you want to go, choose how to get there, and before you know it you're sat around the pool sipping a daiquiri. I blame this on celebrity culture. Down the corner shop every other magazine front cover had another pregnant actress or reality TV star emblazoned across it – some not even pregnant yet, just boldly stating that they were trying. So we figured that if people were that in your face about conceiving, it would be straightforward for us too. Right?

But just for fun, I did a quick Google and it turned out that anything between a few months and a year was the norm. (The NHS website, by the way, helpfully suggests that 'regular sex' will help if you are trying to conceive. I expect elsewhere they also suggest 'drinking water' for those who are thirsty.)

So in the first couple of months of trying, I wasn't too bothered about succeeding. I saw no reason to rush to our destination when the commute was so much fun, albeit militant.

Every time my wife declared it 'leak week' in our house I silently gave my swimmers a little fist pump – this gave me at least another month to try and become a grown-up, bank an entire month's sleep and wave goodbye to drinking. Plus, we were having more sex than Russell Brand in a Viagra warehouse, and, despite it all being steered towards conception, it was tonnes of fun.

As project manager, Rachel was keen to discuss our progress or lack thereof from the start, but I was happy to avoid any heavy conversations early on, like a tardy employee dodging their appraisal:

'Thanks for attending this three-month sex performance review, Mr Avery. I've got some questions for you; please be as honest as you can. Let's start at the beginning: how do you feel you're getting on in the role so far?'

'Well, I believe I've brought a renewed energy to the role and what I've lacked in ability I've definitely made up for with enthusiasm.'

'Okay. Next question: can you highlight an area you feel that you've really excelled in?'

'Last Tuesday in the spare room? I showed that I'm a real team player – you got cramp in your foot and I offered to change position instantly, no questions asked.'

'Right. Final question: is there anything you feel you could have done better?'

'Hmm. I suppose I finished a bit early on Friday so I'll try to make up the time this week instead.'

By the four-month mark, Rachel was starting to panic. We were in Starbucks one busy Saturday afternoon; we'd just bought our drinks and the place was full, so we squeezed into a booth occupied by a little old lady in her 70s. She was wrapped in a striking pink cardigan and beamed a huge smile as she realised she was getting company. I hadn't even removed my coat when Rachel was off.

'What if we can't conceive?' she yelped. 'What then?'

I nearly spat my macchiato down the lady's cardigan.

'We've only been trying for a few months,' I whispered, hoping Rachel would follow suit. 'These things take time.'

'It didn't take Susan and John long,' she responded. (Susan and John are some of our smug-married-couple friends.) She was getting even louder. 'Or the Jacksons. Siobhan got pregnant at her own wedding, before they came back downstairs for the evening do.'

The cardigan lady's eyes had lit up like fireworks. She was now taking a keen interest in our conversation, and I couldn't blame her. This was prime-time juicy gossip for the girls back at the bingo, and she had a front-row seat. I smiled at her uncomfortably and quickly turned back to face my slightly flustered wife.

'Babe. Can we discuss this later?'

'No, because we'll be having sex later. I think we should double the dose.'

The elderly lady nodded her head in agreement. What the fuck was going on here?

'I'm sorry,' I said to the cardigan lady. 'We're trying to start a family and—'

She cut me off by placing her little old hand on top of mine and raising her other to show she was about to make a point. I don't know what I was expecting but it certainly wasn't what came out of her mouth. In an incredibly posh

Home Counties accent she said, 'My Bob, God bless him, used to squash his meat and potatoes together down there. We got nowhere. As soon as he bought some bigger pants we had seven babies. Get yourself some bigger pants.'

And with that, she smiled, stood up, squeezed herself out of the booth and disappeared into the rainy afternoon, no doubt to dish out some more procreation tips to unsuspecting strangers. We finished our coffees and then I nipped into Next for some massive boxer shorts.

Not being able to conceive had been an irrational concern of mine in my 20s, but it hadn't mattered then so I'd brushed it under the same carpet as 'I wonder if I'll go bald?' and 'Will an Additional Voluntary Contributions pension offer enough financial protection upon retirement?' But it returned with a vengeance when after five months we still weren't pregnant. Some months Rachel was several days late, and although we never voiced any excitement to each other, we were both quietly disappointed when it turned out to be a cruel joke from Mother Nature. A bit like when you think you've won a toy on one of those grabby hand games, only for the bastard thing to follow its predetermined programming and drop the teddy bear, all but flipping you the finger as it does. Once she was a full week late and we were both convinced that was it. When her period arrived we were gutted. It felt weird to mourn the loss of something that didn't ever exist in the first place, even if just for a few hours. We went for a walk that afternoon and Rachel admitted that her dormant fears were now being awakened with every pregnancy-free month that passed. I held her hand and told her that everything would be okay, based on nothing but wishful thinking.

I started to get more anxious and quite annoyed at my sperm. With over 40 million of the little buggers involved in each attempt I couldn't help but feel a little let down. Given the opportunity I would have liked to have given them a piece of my mind, like an angry drill sergeant.

'You all know why you're here. ONE JOB you had. The ONLY JOB, in fact, you've been put here to perform. And when it comes down to it, when each and every one of you is representing THESE very testicles, NOT ONE of you can be bothered to actually complete your mission. How would you like to end up like previous alumni? Bouncing off solid rubber walls and getting flushed down the toilet? You don't realise how lucky you are. If this was 20 years ago you'd probably spend your final breaths inside an old sock. So I'm going to tell you one last time, make it count. NOW LET'S GET OUT THERE AND IMPREGNATE!'

Six months passed. Having spent it liberally carpet bombing the target area and hoping to hit the jackpot we decided to try a more tactical approach. It was time to send in the stealth bombers. (I realise this sounds very much as if we borrowed another man's penis, but we instead opted to employ modern-day science.)

Rachel bought some ovulation sticks that were supposed to suggest the most fruitful times for 'relations', and I down-loaded an app on my iPhone. This had loads of 'in-app purchases' that looked like a rip-off, but thankfully the ovulation sticks were much more cost-effective and just required being whazzed on. (After carefully washing her hands) Rachel read out our predictions for the most effective days to procreate – or 'leave it in' as I romantically dubbed it.

As sex moved slowly from pastime towards chore, the act itself did start to lose some of its previous grandeur. Post-sex you shouldn't feel the same sense of accomplishment as when you've mopped the kitchen floor, but often I'd look at my wife and think, *Well, that won't need doing for another few days now.*

Our foreplay, previously so loving and passionate, had been slowly downsized to a quick nod of the head while one of us swiftly drew the curtains. One night we had planned to both watch a movie and have a quick fumble and I was a little careless with my language while suggesting a plan of action.

'If we get *that* out of the way first, then we can relax and enjoy the film.'

I had just referred to our lovemaking as something to 'get out of the way', like we were moving a fridge. Whoops. I waited for Rachel to pull me up on it.

'Good idea,' she said, undoing her top and speed-walking up the stairs.

As a man, one of my key goals during intercourse has always been to try to prolong it as much as possible, and I'll be honest, my results over the years have been quite mixed. I didn't think this was as important while we were trying, but then I read that the female orgasm may actually *increase* the chances of insemination. There are two schools of thought around this. One is that the female orgasm helps the woman to fall asleep post-sex, giving the man's 'baby gravy' a smooth passage. In lieu of an orgasm I did consider lecturing Rachel on my top five motorway service stations, confident that would also have the desired effect.

The alternative premise is what scientific circles refer to as the 'upsuck theory', where contractions of the uterus help to suck the 'love potion' up to its destination, like a procreative Dyson. This quest for the female orgasm led to me asking Rachel to head upstairs and 'start without me' a few times. She always laughed. I was never joking.

Thankfully during the sometimes painful, often joyless, and all too regularly impersonal sex, we never flipped out on each other like we did when trying to construct other things as a couple. Maybe you're more chilled out but for us, stage eight of any flat-pack furniture instructions tends to be 'Discuss divorce with partner.' At least during the latter stage of baby-making there were none of the usual arguments about what goes where, who's holding what and wondering how the all-important screw has gone missing.

One night after all the scheduled and regimented love-making we found ourselves having a long discussion about life and what it all means and then getting carried away in a hug that somehow turned a bit steamy, and before we knew it we were taking our clothes off in the kitchen as I lifted her onto the kitchen counter. Just as we were about to have some of the most pornographic sex of my life, Rachel mumbled in my ear.

'Stop, please stop.'

She must want to go upstairs, I thought. It wasn't the most convenient of locations for a quick fumble, even though having sex in the kitchen had been on my bucket list for a while.

'It's the wrong day,' she whispered.

'But you said Monday.'

'I said Thursday. Save it for then.'

'I can't maintain an erection for three days!'

'Just keep those little fellas ready for me.'

My little fellas had already put on their coats and booked an Uber.

To instruct my legions of semen to stand down and go back to their barracks I opted for the tried-and-tested ice-cold-shower method, although halfway through I started to worry about the effect of ice-cold water on my testicles. Not only were they shrinking like a pair of slugs in a salt mine, but the one on the right seemed to be scaling my stomach to reach the armpit. Two minutes previously I'd been about to give my wife the most effective three minutes in the kitchen since I'd made a Pot Noodle using the hot tap instead of the kettle, and now I was stood with my head under a cold shower jet. I felt like I'd just woken up from an erotic dream.

I read up on the subject (of conceiving – not how to keep an erection for three days) and one of the recurring themes was that you should try to stay relaxed. Why is the advice for pretty much everything nowadays to 'just relax'? Relaxing can be really hard to do. Reader – look away if you're incredibly zen and currently reading this book on a Buddhist yoga retreat in the Swiss Alps. Although I highly doubt that a title such as *Confessions of a Learner*

Parent is on the reading lists of those establishments. If you're anything like me you're much more likely to be found swearing at inanimate objects than perfecting your downward-facing dog.

And from a male perspective, you most definitely don't want certain parts of your body to 'stay relaxed' as that makes the entire process rather impossible (although there is a technique in the tantric yoga community known as 'soft-entry' which is meant to enhance sensitivity in the penis as you wait for the 'dough to rise' in a manner of speaking. We didn't try that . . .). In the end, I translated 'stay relaxed' as 'have a glass of wine' which was much easier to achieve.

Everyone Else is Pregnant So Why Aren't We?

We had reached the seventh month of trying to conceive. By now we'd had several conversations about our fears and worries. Publicly we'd agreed to delay any genuine concern until we got to 12 months, but privately we were both starting to fret. After all, neither of us had accidentally got pregnant or made anyone else pregnant in our combined 57 years on the planet, so it must be us, right?

The unease wasn't helped by seemingly everyone in the world around us getting pregnant. Friends, family and characters on *EastEnders* all welcomed the pitter-patter of tiny feet in what seemed to be a newborn epidemic. Even next door's cat got up the duff twice during our botched baby-making attempts.

The week before I'd been on a night out (remember them?) and got chatting to a friend of a friend who had six kids by three different women. Parking my moral judgement for one second, it was clear this guy was more fertile than a wet gremlin. I didn't know the chap well, but I'd had a few beers so figured I'd just ask him what his secret was. He didn't dodge the question.

'Honestly, mate? Every single time I've got anyone up the duff, I've been absolutely shitfaced.'

I doubted this technique was endorsed by the *British Medical Journal*, but I was already tipsy so wondered what harm it could do. Being sober hadn't worked, so I reasoned that a few million sperm off their tits on vodka Red Bull would at least have a different plan of attack. Unless, of course, they stopped for a kebab when they got to the fallopian tube.

I necked another Jägerbomb and texted Rachel.

FANCY SOME HOT LOVIN WHEN I GET HOME? X

Her reply was typically acerbic.

WHY, ARE YOU BRINGING SOMEONE ELSE HOME WITH YOU?

I learned a valuable lesson later that evening: when alcohol is involved, lovemaking is only a fair fight if both parties have partaken. I was so drunk I could barely get my key in the door – a perfect metaphor for my sexual technique that night. I took my clothes off on the landing and flung the bedroom door open, expecting Rachel to be coquettishly waiting for me like my very own Bond girl. Instead she was fast asleep. I don't remember much of what happened next so I've asked Rachel to fill in the blanks:

'Sam was totally leathered. I woke up to see his bare arse in front of me and I thought he was going to pee in the wardrobe again (he's got form). So I shouted out to ask what he was doing and he turned round, nearly lost his footing and slurred, "Come on, babe. Let's do some sex."

Normally there was no chance I'd let him near me in that condition but as we were trying for a baby I thought we might as well have a go. We started kissing but his breath stank of garlic and Red Bull so we changed position and had less than two minutes of bumbling, incompetent, highly unenjoyable sex. He was snoring into his pillow before I'd finished the bicycle kicks.

'Revenge was mine the next morning though – he was hungover to hell and I insisted on another quickie. I think he puked up not long after.'

What a team we had become!

Thankfully neither of those sessions worked (no one wants the story of their children's conception to involve bad breath or retching). More ovulation red-letter days were put in the diary, but this time we didn't drink for the full week before and we stayed off coffee on that particular day – which caused Rachel to have headaches and gave me a short temper (not normally conducive to effective lovemaking, but it did give me some new moves between the sheets. Not good ones necessarily, Rachel was quick to point out, but definitely new).

It was now August – eight months into Project Baby. Nothing was happening. I felt shattered. Physically, mentally and sexually. The nagging doubt that it was never going to happen was growing bigger each month. When we'd met the lovely old cardigan-lady in Starbucks it had been a mumble; now it was the talking-annoyingly-loud-on-the-phone-on-the-train kind of voice. Rachel and I discussed what life would be like if we couldn't conceive and we both decided it wouldn't be so bad. We'd have each other after all, and we'd be able to afford nice clothes and a decent holiday every year. But despite finding plenty of ways to spin this, it wasn't what we wanted.

But our luck was about to change.

I was taking a stand-up show to the Edinburgh Festival, and we'd been fortunate enough to get tickets for some events at the Commonwealth Games in Glasgow the week prior. We managed to see Usain Bolt in the 4 x 100 metres. It made me giddy to witness the fastest man in recorded history sprint right past me as I struggled with a hot sausage roll I'd hastily bought on the way back from the toilet.

Over the rapturous Glaswegian crowd I shouted in my wife's ear, 'I know it was less than 10 seconds, but that was incredible!'

'Reminds me of last night, darling. But without the last bit.'

Whilst we were in Edinburgh we went for dinner with friends of ours, Karen and Dom, who told us that Karen was pregnant. I used to play squash with Dom and he'd always wiped the floor with me. We hadn't played for over a year but clearly the friendly competitive spirit was still residing somewhere deep within my loins, as that was the night we did it! We finally conceived! 'Let the sperm meet the ovum!' as Paddy McGuinness would no doubt have said if he'd been there.

And with twins. Which made it 2–1, Dom.

(Not that we knew that at the time.)

Bullseye! (and Other Macho Sentiments)

It's the end of August and I'm preparing to travel home from the Edinburgh Festival. I'm up at the crack of dawn to collect my hire car, and once it's loaded, my road buddy fellow comic, Adam, and I are on the A1, talking about the highs and lows of the festival and our plans for the next year.

Now, I doubt that many couples talk about menstruation in depth that often. When you're trying to make babies, though, it becomes as common a subject for discussion as the British weather:

'Is it cold outside?'

'No, but I have just come on my period.'

Every belly-ache, every twinge, I'd convince myself that this was a baby starting to form inside my wife. Sometimes it was just the spicy food she'd eaten. Once it turned out to be a massive trump. I'm not sure you can actually feel the initial formations of a fetus anyway, unless you're one of the X-Men.

But as Adam and I whizz past Carlisle I half remember that Rachel hasn't told me she's had her period in what seems like ages. At least I don't think she has.

Interesting.

I consider bringing it up with Adam but then decide that's only one stop away from being one of those weirdos who tells you they've started 'trying properly'.

Nah, I'll keep it to myself, I think.

We hit traffic on the M6 and I text Rachel at the next services to say we've been delayed, and she rings me instantly demanding to know what time I'll be home. But not in an angry way – there is something in her voice. A twinkle.

By the time we get onto the final stretch of the M62 I'm picking out names and planning how to announce it on Facebook.

I drop Adam off, arrive home, and Rachel gives me a kind of hug I've not had before. It's not just a 'welcome home' hug, it's sweeter than that. Like when someone puts an extra sugar in your tea.

This is definitely it! She's going to tell me, I'm sure! She sits me down on the sofa and reveals she's got something special to welcome me back home with.

Here we go!

I take a deep breath and get ready for the best moment of my life.

She slowly reaches down the side of the sofa with the stagecraft of a Vegas magician – and whips out a gift bag.

What's going on?

I poke my hand inside and pull out a watch box.

She's bought me a watch. I've been driving 90mph down the motorway for a fucking watch.

I can't believe it. Sometimes a knock-back takes the wind out of your sails but mine feel like they've been hacked to shreds and set on fire by a gang of Somalian pirates.

I plaster on a fake smile, like you do at Christmas when your nan buys you a uni-slipper, and open the box. Inside is a pregnancy test. It's positive. We are going to be parents.

What a beautiful swerve.

I could say a number of momentous things to my wife in this moment and express any manner of heartfelt sentiments to the beautiful love of my life who is now carrying our child. Maybe something about the happiness and excitement that is welling up inside me. Perhaps a further declaration of my total devotion to her.

But out of all the options that my brain makes available, my mouth plumps for 'HAVE YOU PISSED ON THIS?!'

We kiss and cuddle and laugh and cry for what seems like ages. I make a joke about not knowing the time because I don't have a watch. Oh, how we laugh.

I grab a bottle of wine to celebrate, realising as I pop the cork that I'll have to drink it all myself.

Ah well.

What's the Story, Morning Sickness?

My mate Rob's wife got pregnant and ran a 10k the following weekend. Rachel got pregnant and I wouldn't even let her run the bath. I was quite envious of other fathers-to-be who just carried on as normal, whereas I transformed into the human equivalent of the Microsoft Office Assistant – that knobhead paperclip character who used to pop up on Word and pester you to let it help: 'Hello! It looks like you're pregnant! Would you like me to mollycoddle you?' It annoyed the shit out of my wife.

The following conversation is typical of those first six weeks of pregnancy:

ME: Do you want a cup of decaffeinated tea, babe?

RACHEL: No thanks.

ME: How about a herbal infusion?

RACHEL: A herbal what?

ME: Infusion. It's a posh name for tea.

RACHEL: I said I don't want tea.

ME: But this is herbal. It's good for you.

RACHEL: I don't want tea. I just told you that.

ME: How about coffee then? I bought some of that lovely decaffeinated stuff.

RACHEL: I don't want coffee either. Especially decaf. It's pointless and tastes funny. Ooh . . .

ME: What's up? What's happening? IS IT THE BABY?

RACHEL: It's my knee. It's itchy. Stop fretting.

ME: Do you want me to scratch it for you?

RACHEL: I can scratch my own knee, darling.

ME: Okay. Sorry. Is there anything else I can do for you?

RACHEL: There is one thing actually.

Finally, a way I can help.

RACHEL: Can you go and sit in a different room, please? You're doing my head in.

Thankfully her cravings for me to bugger off were quickly replaced by the more traditional cravings for food. Blueberry muffins and chip-shop gravy (not together) were particular favourites, although I was slightly disappointed that she didn't hanker after anything downright outlandish like Sudocrem on toast or coal stroganoff. The weirdest one she had was a sudden urge to drink the old water from inside a hot water bottle. One slightly frantic search on the Mumsnet forums later, it appeared that a craving for rubber wasn't even that uncommon in pregnant women. I joked that maybe her yearning for rubber was due to wishing we'd used a condom at the conception, but she picked up the scissors and gave me a funny look so I quickly put my shoes on and headed back to the shop to replenish the muffin stocks.

She was also completely wiped out by 8 p.m. every night, but was having trouble sleeping. She didn't feel sparkling or shimmering, glowing or glittering or, indeed, any of the other clichéd adjectives used for women with child. She felt bloated, hot and uncomfortable. And this was just the beginning.

At about six weeks, the nausea arrived, suddenly and without warning.

She started retching in the bathroom every morning. I'd show support by walking in and shouting 'Are you alright?' over the sound of the shower.

'Of course I'm not alright!'

'Let me hold your hair.'

'I've got a shower cap on!'

It got to the point that we were leaving the house late every morning because she'd have to dash upstairs for one last spew.

Our modern, superficial culture tends to turn a blind eye to the difficult parts of pregnancy. I'd love to see *Hello!* magazine run an interview with the latest *TOWIE* star admitting, 'I was SO pregnant I couldn't shit properly!'

As we all know, it's advisable not to share your happy news with anyone until after the 12-week scan. But Rachel was spending so much time in the office bathroom, and smuggling mints into every meeting, that she became worried that her workplace would think she'd developed a drink problem, so she had to spill the beans early. She also opted to tell the friends she was about to visit out-of-town, reasoning that the instant she refused a glass of wine they'd figure it out anyway. As her workplace and friends were going to find out early, it was only proper that we told our parents first.

We popped round to my mum and dad's one evening and tried our best to drop some hints, figuring it was more fun that way. Mum opened a bottle of wine and we started to tease the big news.

'I'll have a glass, please, Mum, but Rachel definitely won't.'

'Okay, love.' She went back to cutting her lasagne.

Rachel piped up: 'Yeah, I'm going to miss the taste of wine for a good while!'

'Well, do you want a cuppa instead, Rach?'

'No thanks, June. I need to drink less caffeine for a while too.'

'A while? How long for?' We were getting nowhere.

'Oh, I don't know, probably about EIGHT MONTHS!'

'We've got some Lucozade somewhere, I think. Dave, go in the garage and have a look, will you?'

The hints were blowing off course like a badly made paper aeroplane. 'MUM! DAD! RACHEL'S PREGNANT!' Okay, not as subtle, but they couldn't ignore that one.

They couldn't have been happier, and we all embraced with smiles and tears, and then had to dart back home early because Rachel was feeling pretty ropey again.

It was starting to feel a bit more real now.

As I soon learned (from my new best friend, the Internet), morning sickness often doesn't do as it's told and just stick to the morning. But Rachel had a different view about why she was getting waves of nausea in both the morning and evening: she absolutely convinced herself it was twins. I told her this was a load of rubbish. Classic old wives' tale nonsense.

So what was next? Surely a medical expert would have to verify our claim of being pregnant before we'd get to meet someone as important as a midwife? Someone who'd undertake a more rigorous test than one that cost £1.49 from Boots?

Apparently not. We called our GP who took us at our word and booked us straight in to see the midwife.

How exciting!

We sat in her little office, feeling slightly bewildered by all the brochures and flyers that surrounded us, just in case we needed a reminder of what we were there for. I reached over and squeezed Rachel's hand and she raised mine up to her mouth and kissed my thumb. As the midwife typed into her computer we shared a few excited smiles like a pair of teenagers. She finished with her computer and spun the chair round to face us.

I'd never met a midwife before but I'd developed an idea in my head of all of them being heavy-set, friendly and resembling Matron in the *Carry On* films.

This one was late 50s, spindly, and had eyes that bore right through you. We were so excited, and Rachel was desperate to get her twin theory in.

'Any morning sickness?'

'Yes! Both in the morning and in the evening!'

'Any twins in the family?'

'YES!'

'Okay. Well, if you're having twins we'll have to check they're not conjoined.'

Say what?

I looked at Rachel; her face reflected mine – mouth open, wide-eyed, dreams squashed. Never mind pissing on our chips, this lady seemed intent on squatting over our Sunday roast and shitting in the gravy. Why would you say this to someone who was pregnant? If we'd made noises about wanting a girl would she have volunteered up the stats for potential hermaphroditic births?

Undeterred by the new expressions of doom and gloom on our faces, the midwife asked us about all the diseases our family had suffered from, and booked us in for our 12-week scan as she shooed us from her office. We'd arrived filled with glee and excitement and left the appointment feeling deflated and terrified.

Gimme, Gimme, Gimme a Scan After Midnight

For many people, the 12-week scan is seen as the official start of the pregnancy. From 12 weeks onwards the risk of miscarriage drops dramatically, so that's traditionally when you announce it to the world and it moves from concept to real life. But, most excitingly, we'd finally get to see our baby on that little monitor – I hadn't been this excited about looking at a screen since the most recent *Star Wars* film came out.

Rachel kept dancing around the house singing, to the tune of 'I'm Coming Out', 'I hope it's twins, doo-doo, I hope it's twi-i-ins!'

I smiled and nodded, but all the time I kept wondering, *WHY THE HELL DOES SHE HOPE IT'S TWINS?!*

Rachel believed that twins would be:

a) the most wonderful journey of our lives
b) a gift

Whereas I was of the impression that two kids at once would be:

a) twice as difficult

b) twice as expensive, and

c) please refer back to points a) and b).

I was desperate to become a dad but I didn't want to become a dad twice in one fell swoop. Learning to drive had been a stressful experience for me but at least when I got my licence I was only behind the wheel of my mum's old £700 Fiesta, not some Lamborghini with more horsepower than the Grand National. From a distance it looked really hard to look after one baby, so the thought of a tag-team rocking up made my heart pound like a drum-and-bass track.

But deep down I never thought she'd be right. The mere idea of it was ridiculous. Like having sausages instead of arms – ridiculous and impossible. Twins? That was something other people dealt with. I knew that multiple births were more common in women over 35 (at that age there's an increase in something called the follicle-stimulating hormone, which basically sends all the decent eggs out at once, as if the womb is having a Black Friday sale), but Rachel was only 31, so there was no chance we'd be having them.

And then 12 weeks arrived. It was time to put our money where our mouths were. Except it wasn't, because there was some industrial action, so actually we ended up having a 14-week scan instead. Here's a play-by-play:

Our scan is scheduled for 9 a.m., the first of the day. Rachel has strict instructions to drink two pints of water and not empty her bladder before we arrive. Nausea, now a constant companion for my poor wife, makes drinking anything in large quantities difficult. I gently encourage her by chanting 'OY! OY! OY!' as she gulps, until she threatens to surgically remove my scrotum with her hair straighteners.

We punch the postcode of the local neighbourhood health centre into the sat-nav and set off. Twenty minutes and just as many cross words later, we're stuck on a housing estate. We pull up outside a concrete shack that wouldn't have looked out of place in *Breaking Bad*.

'Imagine if *that* was the health centre,' I joke.

We check the sat-nav. It *is* the health centre. Blimey.

We shuffle in and take our seats. 9 a.m. comes and goes. The sonographer is stuck on the motorway, so the waiting room is slowly filling up with pregnant women and their partners, all looking nervous and bursting for a slash. I've had a large coffee this morning so I'm pretty desperate for the toilet too, although I manage to hold it in to show solidarity with my new sisters-in-arms.

After 45 minutes the scene resembles a Japanese endurance-style game show, with bladders swelling to a ridiculous and dangerous level in 50% of the waiting room. This leads to every new person through the door being eyeballed by the piss-heavy queue of hormone-riddled ladies, hoping that each new entrant will be the sonographer.

Eventually a scruffy long-haired guy with a beard meanders into the room, looking like he's late for his methadone prescription. My wife whispers to me, 'Ha! Imagine if it's *that* guy!'

It *is* that guy.

Double blimey.

He calls our names and we abruptly stop giggling and shuffle into his room like naughty schoolkids. He turns out to be an absolute gent, professional, funny and reassuring with it. Rachel lies back on the bed and I perch on a rickety chair next to her. She grips my hand tighter than an arresting officer and shoots me a nervous smile.

The sonographer politely suggests that Rachel might want to take her coat off first, and when she's back on the bed, he squeezes the gel onto his hand and SPLODGE – it's all over her belly and he's already got the scanner in his hand.

Hold on! Where was all the build-up? I was expecting a conversation or some background information so I could acclimatise before we got to the main event, but this whole procedure is more business-like than some of our baby-making sessions. It feels like we're on a rollercoaster without the upwards incline, just sitting at the top ready to hurtle downwards.

I take a deep breath. Every time I think this whole mad escapade has already become real it seems to get even more palpable.

After a few seconds of searching, during which I begin to wonder if it is actually real or just a small misunderstanding, he finds the baby.

My heart rate doubles and I stare at the screen, mouth open. Rachel squeezes my hand and gives me one of her famous smiles that her entire face joins in on.

I am looking at our baby. The image is so nondescript, so black and white and difficult to make out. But it's beautiful. I fall instantly in love with the blurry image in front of me. Time stands still until Rachel gives my hand another squeeze and jolts me back into the room.

'Is there just one in there?' she asks innocently.

I try to convey to Rachel via a complex series of

hand-squeezes that this question is not relevant. Can't we just enjoy this first moment with our little baby? There's a slight pause from the sonographer so I'm confident and relieved that he didn't hear the question.

'NOPE!' he yelps as he moves the scanner to reveal another little guy, in the same way the cameraman does on *University Challenge* when a contestant buzzes for an answer.

And just like when I'm watching that particular show, I feel confused and out of my depth.

FUCK.

My brain disintegrates and my face starts to melt.

Somehow, in the midst of the explosion that has gone off between my ears, my brain manages to stagger out of the smoke, bent double and coughing to form some genuine thoughts. Nothing normal or logical, you understand. In fact, if your normal thought process is fibre-optic broadband, mine had jolted back to resemble a dial-up modem from 2002.

WHAT THE FUCK?

We can't afford this.

I'll probably be waking up any second now.

Best. News. Ever.

Is this really happening?

Hang on – what?

THIS IS AWESOME.

What the actual fuck?

I'M SO HAPPY.

My sperm must be majestic.

I'm not proud of thinking the last one, but it enters my head because deep down I'm a macho idiot. (Later on I will discover that I actually had nothing to do with it, as our identical twins were down to the egg splitting during fertilisation. This ego-blow will be softened by the fact that I'm a big fan of omelettes.)

We are going to have twins. Rachel has been right all along.

Her gut instinct has been vindicated.

Or has it?

It's only prudent to nervously ask him, 'Is there just two in there?' The way I see it, there's an extra baby appearing here every five or so seconds.

He looks me dead in the eye and smiles, as he slowly shakes his head to indicate there aren't just two babies. I'm going to become the father of triplets.

The colour completely drains from my face. Then he says, 'I'm only messing – it's twins.'

Jesus.

'Any thoughts on names?' he asks. Despite arriving late for his own surgery, this guy doesn't hang about. Neither of us can summon the power of speech so he fills the silence for us.

'I had a woman in here once who called her twins Dolce and Gabbana. Isn't that awful? Even T.K. and Maxx would have been better.'

His jokes deserve a better reception, but all we can do is stare, open-mouthed. We walk out of the sonographer's office, holding both the scan pictures and each other closely. Everyone in the waiting room turns their heads to look at us, waiting for a reaction. Many of them look concerned as our faces tell a fairly grisly story. As the whole room holds its breath, Rachel slowly holds the scan picture up for everyone to see, like Rafiki holding Simba up in the opening credits of *The Lion King*.

'There's two of them. Erm . . .' Her sentence tails off, and, like a scene straight from an American sitcom, everyone in the waiting room starts applauding.

Despite trying to wrap our heads around it, it was clear that other people were going to be thrilled if this sample group of complete strangers was anything to go by. We left the waiting room overcome with a curious mixture of emotions. Excited? Definitely. Elated? Absolutely. I was also terrified about our lives spiralling out of control.

'What a gift,' Rachel whispered.

A gift that's twice as hard and twice as expensive, I thought.

'We can tell people now!' Rachel shrieked.

'Let's have a wee first, hey?'

After we'd visited the facilities, we walked out of the health centre slowly and I put my arm around Rachel. It probably appeared to be a show of affection but the truth was I just needed something to prop me up, even if it was a woman pregnant with twins.

Twins?

'I told you!' she said smugly.

'Are you okay?' I asked.

'I'm not sure. Are you?'

'I will be. In a minute. Twins?'

'He definitely said twins, didn't he?'

As two grown-ups who were about to become parents, we dealt with this earth-shattering news appropriately – by cackling in the street. It was a nervous laughter though, the kind when you're getting told off in school and get the giggles.

We sat in the car with my phone on hands-free and called my mum.

'Is the baby okay?' Mum asked.

We paused and smiled at each other.

'They're BOTH fine,' we replied, in vomit-inducing unison (Rachel then opened the car door to actually vomit).

My mum made a noise I'd never heard a human being make before, so high-pitched I think only dogs caught parts of it.

I'm sure all parents agree that there are numerous emotions that explode in your brain like flustered fireworks when it finally sinks in that you're having a baby. They all *look* familiar, but since you last saw them they've been drinking heavily and smashing down a course of illegal steroids and now you can't control them. Happiness is leaning at the bar, giggling maniacally like Heath Ledger's Joker while he pours himself another Scotch. Excitement has become a wild animal and is spinning round in circles, knocking drinks over everyone. Meanwhile Fear has learned to project his voice and is stood on the table in the corner, shouting out random horrible possibilities that will never come true . . . This dive bar of emotions was mushing about in my stomach to create a volatile cocktail that I wasn't sure how to manage. For at least two days, the screensaver in my mind just repeated the mantra: *We're having twins. We're having twins. We're having twins.*

And all I could say out loud was a selection of celebratory swearwords.

Family Planning

Maybe you've just discovered you're going to be a parent for the first time – if so, congratulations! But keep those celebrations brief as there's a fuck-tonne of planning to be done before they arrive. Much of that is practical – I'll get on to that shortly – but first of all you need to wrap your head around just what the hell is going on.

For a start, say goodbye to lie-ins. They'll be in the past, much like bell-bottoms and Blockbuster Video. Post-kids, I once told my childless friend I'd had an 'amazing lie-in until 7.30 a.m.' and he pissed himself laughing. I was deadly serious.

Every time you have a night out before your child arrives you think, *Wow, this might be the last time I get drunk for years*, which isn't true. Your alcohol tolerance will drop so dramatically you'll be absolutely shitfaced when your baby is six months old and you have a large glass of wine.

You'll also start to worry about the following things:

Dressing them

Are they too hot? Are they too cold? It's easier to get into Oxford or Cambridge than to get them into some of their sleepsuits, so you're bound to balls things up a few times. I proudly presented our two to the health visitor at six weeks old with their arms in the leg bits and vice versa. (Don't worry, apart from me feeling like a dick for 20 minutes, no harm was done.)

Dropping them
Yeah, don't do that.

Getting puked on
Some days you'll look like you've been attacked by a flock of seagulls with irritable bowel syndrome. Invest in a baby-sick-coloured sofa and you'll be fine.

Getting pissed on
Newborn babies wee every 20 minutes and this tends to nicely coincide with the moment you hold them in front of your face. Learn to keep your eyes open and your mouth closed.

Getting shat on
The most disgusting part of being a parent is that you're going to end up with more shit on your hands than a clumsy proctologist. Be warned: the first time it happens you will feel violated. By the 100th time it happens it will feel completely normal. Now that is weird.

Unfortunately, just as I was already worrying about all those things, I then had to readjust to accept that I was going to have to worry about all of those things twice.

Everything was going to be more difficult. EVERYTHING. Rachel and I spent hours one night late in the pregnancy just trying to figure out how on earth we would bath them on our own.

'So, there's two of them and one of us. You can't leave one in the bath unattended, clearly. And you can't take them out simultaneously, can you?'

It was beginning to sound like that old riddle with the fox and chicken on the desert island.

'You could always drain the bath while they're still in it. That might make it easier.'

We were discussing our unborn babies like canal boats in a lock.

To me, offspring were like bottles of wine – one's not enough and three is too many. Two seemed like the perfect number, although not when they were due to arrive simultaneously. Stats on British families seem to concur, with the average number of children dropping from 2.42 at its peak down to a slightly more modest 1.92 nowadays. More effective birth control has obviously played a part in this, but don't forget that in the 1950s they didn't have Amazon Prime or Twitter, and these days there's simply no need to procreate just to pass the time.

Friends, family and complete strangers were thrilled for us, wheeling out platitudes like 'Double blessing!' 'Instant family!' Everyone was elated, but then they weren't the ones who'd be dealing with the hard-faced reality of parental ground warfare. They'd all be miles away, popping in for a quick cuddle and a cuppa, while we'd be on the front line contracting tinnitus and trench foot. I went to see Gary, one of my best mates who'd just become a dad himself, knowing he'd be completely honest with me. He looked me in the eye and in his soft Irish brogue whispered, 'You're completely screwed. You know that don't you?'

An Arm and a Leg

Despite his words of 'encouragement', Gary did give me a book he'd read called *The Expectant Dad's Handbook*, which was full of practical advice (although most of which I'd already picked up at the antenatal classes). We also ended up with three copies of *A Contented House With Twins* by Gina Ford and Alice Beer, all of them gifts and all of them offloaded at the local charity shop when I realised that one of the authors didn't even have twins. Whilst not disputing her qualifications as a child expert, I'd much rather take my advice from someone who'd seen action. You wouldn't seek armed combat tips from a Boy Scout, would you?

So after your head has got used to the idea that your baby (or babies) is on its way, your home then needs to follow suit.

Unless you're incredibly New Age and can give your baby all they need with just your nipples and a couple of cloth nappies, pregnancy is the time to tool the fuck up. I've already described parenthood as warfare and preparing for it is your very own arms race. You stockpile every piece of ammunition and firepower you can muster that will keep your baby safe and healthy – and hopefully carve out a victory on the battlefield.

I've lost count of the number of U-turns I've made since becoming a parent, but the first of many came on the equipment. At first I was adamant it had to be brand new. *My kids are going to have all the BEST stuff. They'll want for nothing.* I didn't have a concrete plan of how we could afford this bold strategy, but it was my brain's reaction to the self-doubt I had about coping with my new role as a dad. My hunter-gatherer genetic instincts told me that *I must provide*, and if my brain couldn't cope with what was happening, maybe my credit card could.

What I learned at this stage is that YOU MUST GET ORGANISED. This isn't Chicago in the 1940s and you're not Miles Davis. You can't just rock up and start improvising. MAKE A LIST. Failure to do so will leave you freaking out like those panic-stricken middle-aged men you see in John Lewis on Christmas Eve.

Obviously, as project manager, it was Rachel who figured this out first, scrolling through the entire internet and getting our baby-essentials list into order.

Essential Purchase No. 1: The Pram

It was a bad place to start because these things have their own language. Pram, pushchair, stroller or buggy – what was the difference? Alternatively you could plump for a 'travel system', which sounded like something Marty McFly would be driving through the space-time continuum. We looked at some pictures online and the only thing we knew for sure was that we didn't want them on top of each other (they were identical twins so it's not like we could even shove the ugly one on the bottom). Short of a specialised *Top Gear* episode for buggies (which I would definitely watch) we just had to go and try some out. Rachel and

I waddled and strolled respectively into Mothercare and started test-driving some of the models.

Nice steering arc.

Impressive handles.

Oh look, a cup holder!

Our favourite was an impressive model that was large enough to accommodate the babies and all their assorted baggage, yet seemed to glide across the floor like a gazelle. It was called the Bugaboo Donkey – a frankly ridiculous name, matched only by the ridiculous price: £1,600. Never mind sky-high, this was in orbit and flicking me Vs.

'Have you got anything cheaper?' I nervously said to the shop assistant, struggling to meet her eyes.

'What's your budget?'

'What have you got for £200?'

She looked around the shop, chewing her pen. 'Hmmm.'

Never a good sign. I felt like I was in Christian Louboutin asking for a pair of Crocs. After a few seconds she asked us to wait as she thought 'there might be something in the back'. I've always been suspicious of anything that's deemed unsuitable to grace a shop floor. Whether it's a pair of trousers or a pint of milk, there's normally a very good reason it's been deemed unfit to be visible to potential customers.

My wife and I exchanged nervous smiles, which were pierced by a metal scratching sound as the shop assistant dragged the only pram in our price range back onto the shop floor. With a massive heave and a sharp exhale of breath she managed to dump it in front of us. Until I saw this thing I wasn't aware that an inanimate object could actually look clinically depressed but this thing looked like it'd had a terrible life.

No doubt if this was a Pixar animated movie called *PRAMS!* then our early misgivings about this ugly contraption would be subverted as we got to know its real inner beauty, and after initial snobbery from the other fancy prams it'd no doubt get accepted as one of the gang and go on to lead them to some madcap victory against their evil nemesis.

But this wasn't a Pixar film. It was Mothercare in a rainy retail park and I could tell by my wife's grimace that she was holding in one of those massive pregnant farts that smell like cabbages.

'I'm not putting our kids in that thing. It looks like it lost a bout on *Robot Wars.*'

The shop assistant had struggled to push it across a smooth surface with no kids in it. Imagine how hard it'd be with twins in. More stubborn than a red-wine stain on your favourite chinos. So my parenting U-turn number one was that *secondhand stuff is absolutely fine.*

(When it comes to hand-me-downs, I'm always reminded of a record shop in Nottingham that advertised all their CDs as 'previously enjoyed'. What a wonderfully creative use of language. For a short while I even referred to my dirty undercrackers in the same way.)

We looked online and found an entire subculture of second hand baby and toddler groups that seemed to sell everything except the babies themselves. The sheer breadth of selection in prams was increasing inexorably, and I could feel my head melting. Black or chrome? Collapsible or folding? Cup holder or flux capacitor? By now I just wanted something we could strap them into, and was on the verge of nipping to B&Q to grab a wheelbarrow and some cable ties when Rachel screamed at me.

'I'VE GOT ONE!'

She was so excited I thought she'd found a golden ticket for Willy Wonka's Chocolate Factory. It was even better: she'd tracked down a second hand Bugaboo Donkey on Gumtree. £800. Still expensive, but much more affordable than the sell-your-internal-organs-on-the-dark-web cost of a brand-new one.

Essential Purchase No. 2: Moses Baskets

Rachel knew exactly what Moses baskets she wanted and found them second hand on Gumtree, now the most visited website in our browsing history. (Shamefully, Domino's Pizza is a very close second.) The downside was that they were in Dumfries – a six-hour round trip. As luck would have it, the seller was visiting Liverpool for a work conference, so we arranged to meet up with him in a dodgy car park one night. My concern about us unwittingly visiting a dogging hotspot thankfully wasn't realised, and we grabbed ourselves another bargain.

Essential Purchase No. 3: Breast Pump

My wife really wanted to breastfeed, but as she poetically explained, 'I'm frigged if I'm walking round with two babies clamped to my tits all day.'

I was pretty excited to check out the breast pumps online, hoping we could choose from models with adventurous names like 'Suction Beast 2000' or 'The Lactation Mama' but rather disappointingly they were all very sensibly titled.

Essential Purchase No. 4: Bottle-Making Machine

We were going to mix the expressed milk with formula so we also needed a bottle machine. I read on pregnancyandbaby.com that bottle-feeding was a good way for the father to bond with the kids, plus it gives mum a little break, so I was definitely in favour. We plumped for the one by Tommee Tippee (I don't know who he is but I bet he's stinking rich) – this gadget came more highly recommended than *Game of Thrones* and made the bottles for you at the correct temperature in just a few seconds, like a baby espresso machine. (I still managed to goof things up bottle-wise on numerous occasions, so without this machine I have no doubt that under my watch, my kids would have starved.)

Essential Purchase No. 5: Bottle Steriliser

Buying the bottle-maker meant we needed to get a steriliser to clean the bottles. Other parents have assured me that cleaning incessantly is a prerequisite for your first child; each one that follows causes a re-evaluation of what standards are actually necessary. My friend Iain said that for his first they washed and sterilised everything. For their second they washed everything, and for their third child they pretty much just wiped necessary objects with a dry cloth. I can only imagine when you have a fourth kid you're feeding them directly from the outside bin.

These were our first kids so naturally we went all OCD on the house like a pair of amphetamine-fueled Cinderellas. I went to Home Bargains and bought a load of bleach. My plan was to scrub the floors to within an inch of their life until not only could you eat your dinner off them but you'd be quite happy to spend your free time giving them a good lick.

Essential Purchase No. 6: Car Seats and Bases

The sad fact about car seats is that they're more expensive than actual cars. But due to recent law changes, you're no longer allowed to stuff your baby into the glove box, so if you drive, you kind of need one. And you can't attach the seat unless you have the correct base. We opted for the bases that could accommodate a variety of different seats as the boys grew – aha, a verifiable tip! – and chose to buy these brand new (#smug).

We also got hoodwinked into buying a bunch of items that turned out to be less useful than a sun hat in Aberdeen. Bumbo seats (designed to make your baby sit up even though their body isn't ready), a wet-wipe warmer (I'm still embarrassed we bought this – imagine the prissy little shit you'd turn into if you never felt a wet wipe at its natural temperature?) and a feeding pillow (just use a cushion) all went straight back on Gumtree.

Before I move on from equipment, I implore you to try everything out BEFORE the babies arrive. Nothing will threaten to send you to an early grave more than struggling to figure out a new gadget while the baby next to you does a scream that Edvard Munch would be proud of. We didn't fit car seats until the night before Rachel got induced, which was a terrible, terrible idea. It was getting dark and Rachel had to shine the torch from her iPhone into the car while I sweated and swore for over an hour before we were confident they were safe. And don't get me started on the pram yet (I'll get to that later in Part 2).

As the due date drew nearer, you couldn't see the floor for all the new equipment. As if the impending arrival of twins wasn't enough to make us jittery, our house was starting to look like a real-life game of Tetris.

Complications

Twins are deemed a higher-risk pregnancy so we were booked in to have scans every fortnight. This wasn't a drag at all, in fact it was great to catch up with our little ones regularly and see how they were doing. We got to know the midwives really well and everyone was so helpful and supportive, giving us so many printouts of the scan pictures that you could barely see our fridge by D-Day.

Rachel was convinced we were having girls, and after nailing her last prediction I was tempted to put some money down with Paddy Power. We set about deciding on names for them, which was much harder than we thought. We wanted the names to match but weren't keen on alliteration. We also wanted to give them middle names, mainly so when they were naughty we'd have their full names to scream across the supermarket. I find an extra couple of syllables of shouting help to get your point across clearly, and also alert other shoppers to your highly polished parenting skills.

We also had to eliminate from the selection process any names that ticked the following boxes:

Ex-partners
Knobheads from school
Liverpool FC players (I support Everton)
Everton FC players (Rachel supports Liverpool)

Manchester United players (see previous two points)
Famous serial killers
Warlords
Any names that rhyme with rude words

We finally came to a decision – Connie and Evelyn. The very next day we found out that Rachel wasn't, in fact, the next Mystic Meg and we were having boys. We had to start again. We liked Ben, and after wracking our brains to find another three-letter one-syllable name (to avoid future conflicts between the siblings) we settled on Zac.

Ben and Zac. Zac and Ben. It had a nice ring to it.

One Sunday afternoon we'd come across one of those newspaper lists of 'Britain's Naughtiest Names' in which Ben was listed at number three. During Rachel's 22-week scan, one of the babies kicked his brother in the face, and as his victim recoiled he appeared to smile. We looked at each other and decided that would be Ben.

At this stage, it's probably only fair of me to give you a little warning that the next few pages are slightly less jovial than what has come so far. We certainly weren't prepared but it needn't be a total shock for you as well.

It's 31st December and Rachel is at 24 weeks. It's our last New Year's Eve before the boys arrive and we have a spectacular night planned – pizza, chocolate and a movie on the sofa. But first we head over to our regular scan to catch up with the boys. There are Christmas trees and decorations dotted about the hospital and we give late Christmas cards to the midwives. It's only been a fortnight since we last saw them but the lads have really developed, and on the black-and-white screen we see their little faces and tiny hands and, as usual, we turn to mush. The most exciting year of our lives is about to begin and the thought of bringing these two babies into the world is making us giddy. Life could not be more perfect if we'd designed it ourselves on some futuristic iPhone app. Rachel lies back on the bed-cum-chair that looks like it belongs at a dentist's, and I perch on the stool next to her. Our midwife, Anne, who feels like an old friend as she's been with us for so many happy moments already, is administering the scan as we make chitter-chatter about the festive period and what we have planned for next year. Mid-sentence, Anne abruptly cuts the small talk and her face becomes suddenly serious. These are the moments in life that you dread. It's very apparent that something is wrong but we can't speak. We freeze up, holding each other's hand. I see the fear on Rachel's face, which jolts me into saying something.

'Is something wrong?' I ask, my voice quivering.

'There's a blockage.'

'Where?'

'In Zac's bowel.'

'And what does that mean?' I'm shaking.

'It means we'll have to fix it.'

Oh my God. Does she mean surgery? What kind of blockage? Is our little boy okay?

She goes to get the consultant, and leaves us in the small scan room just the two of us, holding our breath, not sure what is happening.

The consultant comes to take a look and there are no smiles and it's all business, and then we're asked to make our way to the room that nobody wants to visit: the one that says 'Counselling' on the door. We're sat on a couple of armchairs with a table in between us and, in true British style, are given weak tea and a plate of biscuits, as if a few Jammie Dodgers are going to make everything okay.

After 20 minutes, in which every single worst-case scenario plays out in our heads, another consultant comes to speak to us and says that it's not an emergency, just 'a bit of plumbing' that is necessary as without it Zac won't be able to feed himself. Zac has duodenal atresia, commonly known as a 'double bubble' – so called because of the two fluid-filled areas in the baby's abdomen that indicate the problem. Only 1 in 10,000 babies are born with this condition. Then he drops the other bombshell – the blockage could be a 'soft marker' for Down's syndrome and there's a 40% chance that both boys will be born with an extra chromosome.

You never know how you'll react to difficult circumstances. We cried for a bit then went to B&Q. We wanted to stay busy.

None of this changed how we felt about the lads or how the pregnancy would progress but it was a massive shock to the system, and despite this meaning there was a 60% chance of the opposite we subconsciously decided to focus on the 'negative' and get our heads around what we thought would be our new future. We spent the evening holding each other in bed while fireworks outside marked the New Year.

We also felt obscenely guilty for our sadness. So what if they had Down's syndrome? They'd still be loved and given every opportunity to flourish, just as they would if they didn't. Part of our fear was caused by our completely uneducated opinion of what Down's syndrome was and the limitations that it places.

We assumed they'd need looking after constantly and would never work or fend for themselves. Some light reading online showed us that wasn't necessarily the case, and after some friends introduced us to their cousin – an 18-year-old lad with Down's who wasn't letting anything stop him – we felt much more hopeful about the future. We were offered a screening where they would test amniotic fluid from the placenta that would conclusively tell us either way, but we chose not to at that stage – Rachel was at 26 weeks by now and it wouldn't have changed anything on our end other than peace of mind. The screening also carried the risk of premature labour. But with Zac's blockage came a huge increase in fluid, which, if not dealt with, could have also brought on a dangerously early labour for Rachel. By 32 weeks the fluid desperately needed draining, so we opted to get the test done at that point.

I can't remember ever feeling as sickly nervous as the day we went to the Women's Hospital to get the results. My wife was lying on the bed with me sat on the chair as the consultant was given an envelope containing our future – everything went into slow motion, like we were at the shittest awards ceremony in history.

Thank God this woman wasn't a fan of reality TV and didn't try to emulate the faux-tension of those shows. Instead, she opened the envelope like a well-trained post-room assistant in one sweeping motion, slapped the results letter on her knee, scanned it like Predator and barked, 'They're fine.'

Relief burst into the room and throat-punched me as Rachel sobbed tears of happiness. The guilt also returned, instantly. When it's your kids, you're going to love them whatever happens.

D Day

We had been told all along that they don't allow twin pregnancies to go full term these days ('they' being the omniscient hospital folk), so we were booked in to be induced at 36 weeks. Rachel kept correcting me that she was 'being induced' as opposed to 'having an induction' – this was childbirth, not a gym membership.

Being induced meant they'd start contractions artificially by inserting a tablet (or pessary) into the vagina, allowing much more control over when labour begins. On average, 1 in 5 labours begin in this way, and although I'd never heard of it before, I know countless people who've tried their hand at homegrown versions by eating curry or having sex. How do people maintain arousal during those late-pregnancy sexual exchanges? Rachel was so bloated and tender towards the end of the pregnancy that any sexual contact would have been so gentle from me it would have been almost apologetic.

There are also those who firmly believe you should 'let the baby choose' (although what if your baby is crap at decisions?), but with Rachel carrying twins and Zac needing his operation, we didn't have much of a choice. Way back when, you could be carrying quadruplets and they'd just let you keep waddling about until the babies decided to poke their heads out, no doubt doing a bit of overtime down the local coal mine while you waited.

Back then, mums-to-be often didn't even *know* they were having multiples until they'd gone through the gargantuan agony of childbirth, only for the midwife to shout 'KEEP GOING! HERE COMES THE OTHER ONE,' thus wrecking both your head *and* vagina.

And all this would be going on while the dad was sitting in the pub with his mates.

It's a given nowadays that the dad should be present at the birth but I'd like to think that even back then I wouldn't have just left my wife to it while I nipped down the local for a few swifties and a game of cards. These were our babies and I wanted to do as much as I could to help my wife in what was turning into a pretty difficult pregnancy.

Rachel had ballooned to the size of a small Zeppelin at this stage and was struggling to walk around. A few times she'd managed to become stuck on her back while trying to get up from the sofa, arms and legs flailing like an upside-down tortoise. I always helped her up as soon as I'd taken a quick snap. She was also forced to start wearing these impossibly huge maternity pants that looked so comfy I even tried them on a few times. Some of her clothes at this point looked like they were crying for help just to stretch over her bump which was now clearly visible on Google Earth. It was all belly, though. No other part of her had increased in size other than her tummy.

(Unless you count her breasts. Her beautiful, plump, irresistible boobs that I was now under strict instructions not to touch on punishment of death. Mother Nature is clearly a massive spoilsport as she gives pregnant ladies the most stunning norks yet makes them completely unbearable to the touch. This left me leering over them like a building-site pervert, knowing that just like the Mountain Laurel flower of North America, as beautiful as they looked, if I touched them I'd probably die.)

It was the eve of 36 weeks, and by now we knew that the boys didn't have any additional chromosomes, but we still had to wrestle with the thought of Zac undergoing major surgery almost straightaway. I told myself I was excited but the truth is I was scared. Terrified, in fact. I'd not met my children yet but they had already redefined what 'love' meant in my understanding (I used to think I 'loved' Jaffa Cakes and *House of Cards*, for instance). I wanted to protect them from anything that could hurt them but at this stage we both felt completely powerless. We were about to touch down into the foreign land of parenthood, but before we could get to the sunny beach we had to collect our luggage (the birth) and navigate our way through passport control (Zac's operation).

I didn't vocalise any of this to Rachel as I wanted to stay strong for her.

The day before the induction was a Sunday so we planned a stereotypical childless Sunday for us, knowing it was our last one. Ever. Fuck. It felt so intense when you said it like that. We had a nice lie-in and then watched some cricket under the duvet with a Domino's.

It was our last night of full sleep yet we managed to get hardly any sleep at all.

I tossed and turned until about 2 a.m. when I woke up in an empty bed. Rachel had gone downstairs and was almost inconsolable. We poured our hearts out and I came clean about how scared I was too.

I get nervous enough when old friends are coming to stay, and they don't tend to stick around for 18 years. They also don't tend to arrive via my wife's vagina. We'd both expected to be excited at this stage – we were just a day (maybe two) away from meeting our little boys for the first time – but the stress of the pregnancy had weighed heavy. Now we were filled with dread, knowing that both babies would be whisked away from us almost immediately, Zac for his operation and Ben to Special Care. We were in a privileged position because we knew exactly when the boys were coming, so this should have been a night of excited chatter and 'this time tomorrow . . .' talk. Instead we spoke of fear; me: of the birth itself, and Rachel: of the separation and subsequent lack of bonding.

We passed out in each other's arms, exhausted.

The next morning, the day is finally here.

6 a.m.

Our alarms go off as we're due at the hospital for 7.30. Despite knowing full well that this is D-day we've somehow neglected to pack anything. Rachel frantically throws a load of PJs and big knickers into a hold-all and I chuck my phone charger, toothbrush and *The Expectant Dad's Handbook* in a Tesco bag.

6.45 a.m.

We're going out the front door. 'Breast pads!' Rachel suddenly shouts (next door's cat stares prudishly at us).

I dash upstairs and grab the packet from the bathroom. I run back down to the front door.

6.47 a.m.
We're getting in the car when Rachel squeaks, 'Maternity pads!' Back in I go. Back down I come. Next door's cat continues to stare.

6.49 a.m.
I pass the maternity pads to Rachel as I get in the car. 'They're waxing strips,' she says. (You don't want to get those mixed up.) I fluster out of the car, through the door, up the stairs, into the bathroom, grab the afore-mentioned 'vadge-pads'. Also spot the pack of flannels we've bought to keep Rachel cool during labour. That's got to be everything!

6.54 a.m.
Back home again. We've not packed any clothes for the boys.

7.25 a.m.
I take a ticket for the car park and wonder how long we'll be there. Hours? Days? Weeks?

7.30 a.m.
We check in at the front desk with all our baggage, literal and emotional.

'Don't say I never treat you to a nice holiday' is my attempt at punctuating the tension but it goes down like an eggy fart in a lift. 'They' tell us we've been earmarked for a certain kind of room, with it being twins. The fly in the ointment is there is a further six-hour wait before we can get in there. As a fervent supporter of the NHS I totally understand – we're not hiring a pedalo here and you can't really hurry these things along. I just wish we could go home and back to bed. People talk about labour being exhausting but we've rocked up to the party with empty tanks already.

9.40 a.m.
Other people waltz up and become parents quicker than most people queue at a deli counter.

10.25 a.m.
One couple turn up with nothing but a bump and a car seat, seemingly carefree. 'I bet they'll be home in time for *Loose Women*,' I say to no one in particular.

1.15 p.m.
Finally, a midwife comes through and calls our name.

She walks us through to the room where everything will change. The room is big, like a squash court, with a bed in the middle and more medical equipment than I've seen in one place before. If we were in a Bond film, I'd expect to see Q walk into shot, demonstrating his latest space-age gadget. It's quite warm but the atmosphere is a little cold, clinical. I suppose you don't want it to feel like a Wacky Warehouse. The nurse says that someone will be in to see us soon and to make ourselves comfortable.

2.20 p.m.

The midwife comes to get the induction started, and treats my wife like a dishwasher, by inserting a tablet into her vagina.

5.10 p.m.

Pretty much nothing has happened. A midwife comes to perform a 'sweep' on my wife, which basically consists of fishing around up inside her to determine if anything is happening. We were hoping for a gentle soul. Ideally someone who'd used a lot of Fairy Liquid in their time and had hands like silk sheets. In the distance I can hear a faint thud, getting ever louder. The glasses of water on the table begin to shake like that scene in *Jurassic Park*.

That's when she arrives. OUR midwife. With hands like rusty shovels and a demeanour that suggests she probably indulges in a bit of bare-knuckle boxing at the weekends. Probably not competitively anymore, mainly just for the sheer fun of hurting people. She gruffly says hello and tells us she's retiring and this is her last-ever shift in the job. Bloody hell. I've left jobs before and when on the home straight you don't tend to give two shits about anything. Mentally, you've already clocked off.

She starts the sweep, which I thought would involve her carefully using her fingers until she was able to get more purchase. But remembering she has a leaving do to attend she just goes straight in with a fisting, like she's trying to find a tennis ball that's got stuck round the back of the garage. She goes so deep at one stage I'm quite concerned she may have lost the watch she's been given to celebrate her retirement.

She does offer us some cake though, which is nice.

Several times during this process Rachel is told to 'just relax' which I'd wager is impossible with a complete stranger up to their elbow in your genitals.

7.30 p.m.

We're starting to feel duped. TV shows have made us believe that labour is a mild discomfort that neatly fits within the body of a 26½ minute installment. Films lie to us even more with movie births often lasting a matter of minutes. With inductions it seems less like a Hollywood action movie and more like a French arthouse flick where fuck-all happens for long periods. I wonder if with a standard birth it would be all action. The waters break, you dash to the hospital and boom! – the baby pirouettes out of your wife's foo-foo and into your arms like a wet rugby ball. I ask the nurse and she tells me most first labours last between six and 12 hours. That means I could fly to Dubai in the same time, or even listen to a full Pink Floyd album.

8.40 p.m.

After the first tablet doesn't work they insert a second. We are convinced that she's clocked off already but OUR midwife arrives for her last-ever task on the job – violently shoving it up my wife like she's trying to put a pound coin into a stubborn pool table.

We continue to wait.

I'm Coming Out

My wife had opted for a natural birth because she didn't want to miss out on the experience. I gently suggested that a C-section might be easier for her. Why take the scenic route when you can jump on the motorway?

We'd been urged to write a birth plan – this would be her wishes for everything during the birth.

It looked like this:

Birth partner: Sam Avery (husband)
Would you like this person to be with you at all times?: Yes
Preferred position: Whatever's comfortable
Drugs: Epidural, please

I'm glad that men don't give birth, mainly because our birth plans would look like this:

Birth partner: Rach (the wife)
Would you like this person to be with you at all times?:
   Probably not
Preferred position: Doggy. Ha! Just joking. #banter
   Whatevs, mate
Pain relief: Carlsberg

I had to memorise Rachel's birth plan because during labour I would become her press secretary and all questions would be fielded by me. To avoid scrambling round for bits of paper in the middle of a crucial moment I spent ages revising for my big test.

Ad break over

(Day Two) 5.15 a.m.

About 14 hours in (still 12 hours to go), one midwife tells me to get my camera ready for the 'big moment'. This has always baffled me. People often ask, *Who is filming their children being born*? But that's not the real question. What I want to know is *who the hell is watching it back*? It's great to have ammunition to embarrass your kids with when they grow up, but I can't see any upside to showing the full birth on a big screen at your daughter's 18th surprise party. I suppose you'd save money on the buffet.

9.50 a.m.

After all the anxious build-up and huge amounts of pain for Rachel, almost no progress occurs for 18½ hours. And I have to admit, it's pretty boring. Rachel can't walk around (she's hooked up to heart-monitoring machines) and making small talk feels a bit weird, so we just sit there. The most excitement we get is when she becomes convinced she needs a poo, but instead it's a really long, baritone fart that sounds like a ferry docking.

I decide to try and finish reading *The Expectant Dad's Handbook* (I couldn't finish it beforehand as I'd been revising the birth plan), which causes a farcical moment when the midwife comes in and sees what I'm reading.

'Bloody hell, you've left it late, haven't you?'

'It's okay,' I assure her. 'I've nearly finished it.'

I'm on page 23. By the time I get to page 178, Rachel is still in early labour.

11.45 a.m.

In an apt foreshadowing of actual parenthood, sleep is impossible. We find more and more mind-numbing ways to pass the time, like playing that alphabet game you often do on long car journeys, the one where you take turns to think of something beginning with each letter of the alphabet.

Rachel made it very clear before we got to the hospital that I was not to make her laugh during the birth. Unfortunately, I tend to deal with stressful situations by making inane and moronic comments so this is becoming a challenge.

'Please, please don't make me laugh,' she repeats.

'Even if you poo the bed?' I decide definitely not to say.

She also tells me that under no circumstances am I to ask questions whenever she has a contraction, as 'Are you okay?' or 'Does that hurt?' will not help, especially if she is in too much pain to answer.

A contraction arrives. It is pretty intense.

'Are you okay?'

'That's a question!'

'Is it?'

'So is that!'

'Sorry! Shit. Erm, let me know if you're okay?'

I suppose anything is a question if you pronounce it a certain way. In the end I just keep my mouth shut for nearly 27 hours as we wait for the twins to arrive. I haven't waited this long to see someone since I went to watch Guns N' Roses in concert aged 14.

1.25 p.m.

My wife slogs through labour with strength, grace and a creative use of the English expletive system. And every time we think we're close, they run a check and tell us that we are at least a couple of hours away from anything happening. By now I've polished off *The Expectant Dad's Handbook* so I inform Rachel that I'm now technically ready for the babies to arrive. She looks at me with more contempt than I could ever describe using merely language (I'd need sound effects and pyrotechnics to do it justice) but thankfully, about 20 minutes later she enters active labour.

5.27 p.m.

Another four hours later, as Rachel reaches the final stages of labour, she is in total agony and asks me to play the alphabet game again. I suggest animals as the category and she screams that it's a shit category. I apologise and under pressure can't think of another one. She howls at me to 'JUST PICK ANOTHER FUCKING CATEGORY!' like some lost out take from *The Exorcist* where they all play parlour games. I panic and suggest we do makes of car instead.

The pain and adrenaline must have taken her to a hyper state of intelligence as she rifles through the entire alphabet without giving me a look-in. I decide not to pull her up on the rules of the game that specifically state you must take turns with the other player, mainly because she is shouting at the top of her lungs again, demanding another category.

5.29 p.m.

In the middle of all this absurdity, the top of Zac's head appears. I move myself down between Rachel's legs – I want to be at the coalface for this momentous occasion even though I'm not entirely sure I want to witness what is about to happen. I force myself to look because I don't want to regret missing anything, but every fibre of my being attempts to shift my gaze to anywhere but Rachel's ever-expanding Grand Canyon.

I brace myself. Here we go. Then Ben's heart rate drops and he goes into distress – perhaps he doesn't want to be left alone in there, even for just a few minutes. The consultant is taking no chances and opts for an emergency C-section.

Turns out 26 hours on the scenic route led directly to the motorway anyway.

5.32 p.m.

The rest of the team appear like a medical flash mob, and general anaesthetic is being administered to Rachel as they explain to me that I can't stay with her for this part. We hurriedly say our goodbyes as I kiss her on the forehead and hold my hand against her cheek for as long as I can until she's wheeled away from me and into surgery. There's a general mood of chaos following her out of the room and for the first time since the 24-week scan I have some seriously dark thoughts. *What if something goes wrong? What if this really is goodbye?*

Rachel looks like a frightened little girl as she disappears from view and I'm ushered into a tiny waiting room that has three chairs and a coffee table with a copy of *Take a Break* magazine. The front cover has the headline 'My Ex's Ghost Got Me Pregnant' which I decide is wholly inappropriate under the circumstances. It comes to me that a good tagline would have been 'He Put the Willies Up Me'. It's strange how your brain deals with stressful situations.

5.37 p.m.
I'm just becoming engrossed in the true-life story of a Gypsy paternity battle on page 7 when the midwife comes running in and tells me I am the father of two beautiful boys.

'Beautiful! So they're not mine?' I un-hilariously quip. She gives me a hug then runs off with my phone to take some pictures. Now, let's be honest here. Newborn babies aren't nearly as cute as they become a few minutes later – like a good roast chicken they need to stand for a minute or two before they're ready. So let's just say that the first photos she showed me most definitely weren't going on our mantelpiece anytime soon.

5.44 p.m.
But then she brings them both into the waiting room for me to hold, beautifully swaddled in white towels, eyes closed like puppies. Puppies that look a bit like me. And that's when it hits me in the gut that this is one of those moments in life that will never leave me, like my wedding day, or that time they opened a new till at Aldi and I managed to scoop up all my shopping in one hand and dive to the front.

Magic.

They are so still and peaceful, their only movements are their teeny, tiny nostrils flaring ever so slightly to take in their first breaths. The midwife leaves the room to give me a moment with them and as my eyes fill up with a joy that I haven't ever felt anything close to, I notice that the blanket on one has moved slightly over his mouth. Parental programming 2.0 kicks in and I think, *I'd better just move that away a bit*, but realise I don't have a free hand to do so. Can I put one of them down? Crap. Can't do that either. Oh shit, one's started wriggling . . .

'MIDWIFE! GET BACK IN HERE!'

Emotionally, this was going to be the most amazing journey of our lives.

Logistically, this was going to be a fucking nightmare.

5 Things I Learned on the Road to Parenthood

1. It's easier to crack the conundrum on the Kazakhstan version of *Countdown* than it is to wrap your head around the fact you've co-created a new human with your genitals.

2. Complete strangers will put their hands on a woman's pregnancy bump and ask searching questions about the conception in the middle of Primark.

3. It's best not to get caught by your wife having a quick snooze during the antenatal yoga class.

4. The drawn out, gruesome labour and the way my wife tackled it means she has now usurped Everton legend Duncan Ferguson as my all-time hero.

5. When your child is born it dawns on you that it'll be well over a decade until your next proper lie-in.

Part 2:

Then There Were Four

Zac's Operation

I was 36 years old and had luckily never needed an operation. Zac had one within 36 hours of being born.

After the birth Ben was taken to Special Care in the Women's Hospital and Zac spent 12 hours there before being transferred to Alder Hey Children's Hospital for his op, about a 20-minute drive away. The operation was to correct a blockage he had between his stomach and his bowel that would otherwise prevent him from feeding properly. The doctors said they would be making an incision around his belly button and disconnecting either side of the blockage to create a new connection.

Thinking back, I was very calm about the whole thing. Waiting for him to go down to theatre wasn't the wrench I thought it would be, as I just convinced myself that he'd be okay. I even joked with the surgeon, when he told me we'd barely be able to see the scar, that it would be great if he could make it noticeable enough so we could tell him apart from his brother. (Most scars seem to look like the letter Z anyway, at least on cartoons.)

So he went down for what was to be a two-hour operation and I went back to the Women's Hospital to see my wife and other son, strangely feeling pretty fine with everything. That was until I got the call that he was out of surgery and doing okay, and then I fell apart quicker than a game of

Jenga on a bus. I don't know where I'd been storing the anxiety and dread but as soon as I knew he'd got through it I felt whatever stoic dam had kept my emotions in check collapse like a piece of soggy Weetabix. Rachel and I sobbed into each other's shoulders as she confessed that she felt like the worst mother in the world.

'It's only your first day,' I countered, like she'd just started a new job.

'I've held him twice and now he's gone away for major surgery in another part of the city and I'm not even there. I've let him down. I've let them both down.'

There was nothing else she could have done – she was bedridden after the C-section and physically couldn't go anywhere near Zac or Ben. I told her that I understood why she felt so crappy about it, but that she was being silly to punish herself as there was nothing she could do.

I didn't discuss this with Rachel but I was now acutely aware of just how *lucky* we were. At Alder Hey earlier that day I'd got chatting to a young mother whose twins had arrived at 24 weeks, with one of them not making it. The other had been in hospital for five months and both parents were staying at the hospital, which meant neither had been to work since the premature birth. There was a strange combination of strength and exhaustion in her eyes and it was mind-blowing. When she asked about Zac's ailments and birth weight (6lb 7oz) I was almost embarrassed telling her – our worries seemed like small fry compared to what she and her young family were going through. (Ben was only 4lb 11oz at birth but has grown into such a generous little boy that we often wonder whether he let Zac have the extra weight for his operation.)

I went back to see Zac that evening, feeling this awful parental sickness in my stomach as I parked the car. These feelings were all new and not enjoyable in the slightest – I was looking forward to watching them at sports day or sticking their first painting to the fridge, not seeing them hooked up to medical machines on day one of their lives.

And at times like this, you look for anything to lift your spirits. I was lucky enough to be sitting in the waiting room this time next to a young dad who was with his three-year-old daughter. He was on the phone and asked the young girl, 'Porsche! Do you want to speak to Mercedes?'

This guy had called his kids Porsche and Mercedes. Wow. Then Porsche took the phone and opened the conversation to Mercedes with 'Hiya, Nan.'

Nan. Awesome.

I went into Zac's room and watched him sleep for about an hour. He looked pretty good for someone just over a day old who'd already gone under general anaesthetic and been sliced open. The staff, all staggeringly helpful, told me that he was on the right track and they'd try to feed him in the morning to see if the op had been a success. I considered signing him up for Tough Mudder, but instead gave him a kiss and headed back to Rachel and Ben.

I hoped that every day as a parent wouldn't be this taxing.

Have a Poo, Poo, Poo (Push Pineapple Shake a Tree)

The next day shot by in a blur, speaking to doctors about Zac and midwives about Ben. I tried to shield Rachel from the detailed medical information but she was obviously desperate to know about all the tests and procedures, despite recovering from the caesarian. There's only so much medical info I can take in before my brain stops digesting it, like when you ask for directions in a foreign town and it just becomes noise. One thing I did understand was that Ben had jaundice, which wasn't a surprise – he was four weeks premature and looked as yellow as a Coldplay hit single. So they stuck him under a phototherapy lamp and monitored his blood sugar, which was going up and down like James Bond's trousers.

I spent the evening back at Alder Hey standing over Zac's incubator talking to him with a lump in my throat. It's amazing how much you can find to say to a three-day-old boy who's not listening. I told myself it was good for him to hear my voice but in reality it was more for my benefit – I needed to feel like I was helping in some way.

The machines he was hooked up to beeped at reassuringly regular intervals, until now and then one would go freestyle and start bashing out some kind of funky jazz riff. This made me panic every time, dashing out to one of the nurses to ask them what it meant. I've watched too many TV shows where the wrong kind of beeping means something catastrophic. Each time they put my mind at rest until I became quite familiar with which noise meant what.

The staff told us that Zac had taken his feeds like he was on an infant version of *Man v. Food*. This was wonderful news, but the big question now was whether he'd digest it properly after his operation. We were basically told to 'pray for poo', which is a part of Sunday school I must have missed.

I imagine most new fathers go out and celebrate the birth of their firstborns with a brandy and a cigar, but as my wife was still in the Women's Hospital, the staff kindly let me stay on a fold-up bed. So instead of wetting the babies' heads in the traditional sense, I smuggled some cheap, warm wine and a plastic camping beaker into our room and drank it in the pitch dark like a dirty squatter. Because if nothing else, I know how to party.

The next morning I was up extra early as I wanted to get myself and the latest breast-milk haul across to Alder Hey before rush hour. You don't want to be stuck in a slow commute with a tube full of colostrum in your pocket. (I became a breast milkman that first week, ferrying some of the good stuff my wife had expressed over to Zac several times a day, and despite not having a milk float I did drive at about the same speed. On my first round I somehow managed to get trapped in the revolving door and nearly poured my shipment all over some posh guy's tweed jacket.

'What's that stain on your Cheviot Harris, Sebastian?'

'Just a bit of nork brew, Margaret. Nothing to worry about . . .')

I arrived filled with hope and dread in equal measure. There'd been no movement yesterday so we were desperate for progress. I carried the milk and a bag packed with nappies and baby clothes as other parents shot me the traditional closed-mouth-with-no-teeth sympathetic smile. Still trying to get to grips with fatherhood added to the fact both my lads were in hospital, I felt like I was living someone else's life.

I buzzed the door of the Neonatal Surgery Unit and tried to read clues about my son's condition from the voice intonation of the guy who answered. The automatic doors swung open, I hung my coat up and squirted enough sanitiser into my hand to cleanse a skunk.

It wasn't a long walk from the unit's front entrance to Zac's room but it took me so long I might as well have been walking uphill into a wind tunnel on a down escalator wearing roller skates. The nurse was inside his room so I took a deep breath, knocked and opened the door.

She looked at me.

Silence.

Then her mouth slowly formed a smile.

'He's had THREE poos! Massive ones too – huge!'

A confetti cannon went off in my head and the room span. Bowel movements often have the ability to make your eyes water but not normally like this. Overjoyed, I phoned my wife and shouted, 'HE'S HAD THREE MASSIVE SHITS!' down the phone. Everyone in the car park turned to stare but I didn't care. The operation had been a success.

No Breast for the Wicked

If breastfeeding is 'the most natural thing in the world' then why is it so hard? I'm not speaking from personal experience although I was tempted to have a quick go on the breast pump when it arrived. I didn't, mainly because I was worried I might cause damage or, God forbid, actually enjoy the experience. And with twins on the way I knew it wasn't the right time to give myself a weird sexual fetish. I'm saving that for my mid-50s.

Rachel was determined to try breastfeeding, or at the very least continue expressing milk for the boys to bottle-feed on. With Zac still in Alder Hey after his operation and Ben over in the Special Care ward, neither was actually with us yet. This was heart-wrenching, as she hadn't seen them both together since the birth.

Before the birth she'd been very pragmatic about breast-feeding – if she could, great. But if she couldn't? Well, it wouldn't matter. That changed as feelings of failure flooded her body, so expressing breast milk became even more important for her to fill the gap in what, as a new mother, she felt was neglect but in reality was necessity – she couldn't leave the Women's Hospital yet as she was still recovering from the caesarean.

I don't think we give caesarean sections the credit they're due. Let's not forget, a C-section is the slicing open of a woman's stomach so wide that we can yank another human out. That's gruesome as heck, hence the usually long recovery period. A highly dangerous element to throw in to that convalescence is an emotion that many new mothers feel in abundance – determination. Rachel's determination to see her kids caused her to collapse in the hospital corridor. To my eternal guilt, I wasn't present, so here she is again, in her own words:

'I woke up at 3 a.m. to try to keep my milk flow going, and I got the most overwhelming urge to go and see Ben. I knew I could wake Sam up and get him to take me round on a wheelchair but he was fast asleep so I thought I'd try to walk round on my own. I struggled to get from the bed to the bathroom normally, so by the time I got to the end of the corridor, my body gave out on me and I slumped to the floor, sobbing. I felt utterly helpless.'

Pretty intense, huh?

But back to breastfeeding. Rachel had the collection syringes near her nipples and was ready to go when I learned another huge lesson: muttering 'Milky, milky' under your breath does not get a woman in the mood to express. The male equivalent would be when that fella who's hung like a donkey comes and stands too close to you at the urinal. You just dry up.

I left the room and in the end she got going, but it wasn't easy. Because breastfeeding mirrors parenting, in that every person you speak to tells you something completely different:

'Rub them really hard.'

'Softly does it.'

'Tickle slowly around the nipple.'

'JUST SLAM 'EM IN THE FRIGGIN' DOOR!'

We were shown various approaches on numerous people's boobs, the pillows and the duvet. One woman we'd never met before came into our hospital room late at night and tried to demonstrate a much more aggressive technique directly onto my wife's chesticles. To this day I'm still not sure she definitely worked there.

Then we got told that BAMBIS (Babies And Mums Breastfeeding Information and Support) were coming in to speak to everyone. The way they were described to me they sounded like a 1970s Nation of Islam style aggressive paramilitary group, bullying women into lactating through brute force. I was waiting to hear them goose-stepping down the hospital corridors while Darth Vader's music played. The truth was that they were the polar opposite – helpful, supportive and friendly, and they really put Rachel's mind at rest.

The only thing that everyone seemed to agree on is that, once again, the woman should be relaxed. This meant that, just as at the birth, my only role was to keep my mouth shut during any feeding attempts. The emotional trampoline we were jumping on was energy-sapping, and our sleep was constantly interrupted by hospital noises and random nighttime visits from midwives, so we kept hitting a wall.

On day three I pushed my wife in an old-skool wheelchair over to have a dab at breastfeeding with Ben in Special Care. I pressed the intercom and giggled like a schoolgirl after saying 'I'm here to see Ben Avery. It's his dad.' The words felt weird in my mouth.

We put those privacy screens up that they use for fixing manholes in the street and got Ben out of his cot. The midwife had suggested it might be a good idea to 'introduce' Ben to the breast first, which I thought sounded a tad formal.

'Ben, this is your mother's breast. Breast, meet Ben.'

'Er, lovely to meet you, Breast. What a nice areola you have. God, I'm sorry, I've never been good at this small-talk stuff. Do you have any sisters? Oh sorry, she's right there. Hi, madam, my name's Ben. My word, are you two twins as well?'

The idea of this was to get him interested in the general area, which I wasn't worried about – I knew if he turned out like his father he'd be listing it on his CV under 'hobbies'. Unfortunately he'd never seen a breast before so when he woke up to one directly in front of his face that was bigger than his head he started to blubber. In that situation I think I'd cry too. (Tears of joy are still tears.)

So Rachel returned to having her nipples and soul sucked dry by the double breast pump. She'd clamp this robotic bastard to her chest four times a day while it chugged away like a sexually depraved Nespresso machine.

This left me feeling desperate to help in some way, so I started washing the evil contraption after each milking session. Being pretty clueless when it came to the sanitation of bosom-based extraction contraptions, on one occasion I ended up washing it three times.

The first wash was pretty thorough so I decided to grab a quick 15-minute nap afterwards, but couldn't relax as in my mind all the germs on the pumps had survived my onslaught and were doing a dirty version of the dance from *Fantasia*. I opened my eyes and noticed a bit of soapy water still on the inside.

I'll give it another once-over.

The second attempt was done with the poise and patience of a bomb-disposal expert. As I carried the pumps back to my wife's bed a midwife casually enquired: 'You didn't use your hands to carry them, did you?'

As opposed to what? Juggle them with my feet like some kind of post natal circus act? Maybe use my as-yet-unproven Jedi abilities to make them float across the room? WHAT THE FUCK DID SHE MEAN?

Of course, what she meant was that I should have carried them in one of those cardboard bowls that people puke in.

So the third clean was fueled by pure anger, which is definitely the most effective emotion for cleaning. I once had a huge row with an ex and vacuumed the entire house in eight minutes flat, corners and sofas included. The added benefit was that the neighbours could only hear my rage-ridden expletives when I turned the Hoover off to change plug sockets.

I tried to stay calm by reasoning that this was the closest I'd get to my wife's boobs for some time but it didn't work. Instead I got a horrific glimpse into what it must be like living with a debilitating form of OCD. I could sense the germs, those evil little bastards jumping around with plans to infect my offspring.

So after the kind of washing normally reserved for a new inmate at Shawshank Prison, this pump was now cleaner than Gary Lineker's disciplinary record. Feeling disproportionately proud, I swaggered back to my wife's room with a look on my face that said *I've just washed a double breast pump three times. Don't mess with me.*

'You're supposed to dry it too you know.'

I trudged back to the hospital utility room knowing that my Saturday nights would never be the same again.

Look Who's Back, Zac

The next day the midwife said my wife could go and visit Zac at Alder Hey. She hadn't seen him since the morning after he was born, so to say it had been difficult for her would be the biggest understatement since an Austrian primary-school teacher wrote 'potential troublemaker' in a certain A. Hitler's school report.

I pushed my wife through the hospital corridors in a wheelchair with her hoodie covering her face, like we were breaking her out of a prison or recreating that scene in *E.T.* In the car I didn't negotiate the speed bumps on the way out as well as I should have – I sped over them like I was evading a police chase, which wasn't good for my wife's brand-spanking-new C-section. She managed to remember some of the swearwords she'd invented during labour, which was both impressive and intimidating – I slowed down so much for the next set of bumps that it seemed like I was driving sarcastically, if that's possible.

The walk from the car to the main entrance at Alder Hey took longer with the pair of us. This visit was emotionally essential but physically exhausting for my wife. It was late by the time we arrived, and the hospital was quiet. We pressed the intercom at the Neonatal Unit and I waved at the security camera when they buzzed us in. The short, slow walk to Zac's room began, the staff beaming at us as they realised what a huge deal this was. The young mother I'd met on my first visit there spotted us through the window to her son's room and we exchanged smiles, her giving us a thumbs-up.

We opened the door to Zac's room and everything went into slow motion. It'd be a cliché to say that the past week's events felt like we were in a film, but at times I'd been expecting to hear a director shout for a retake – quite a few of the scenes had felt like bad outtakes from a Ken Loach misery-fest. This was much more Hollywood – in fact, the post-production team in my memory banks have already put this moment into soft focus with a classical music score.

Rachel picked him up out of his incubator and cradled him with tears streaming down her face. He was still connected to two machines, which made the embrace slightly awkward, but only physically – a serenity washed over his tiny face as he heard his mother's voice for the first time in a week. She fed and winded him and gave him a week's worth of cuddles in the three hours we spent there, and then it was time to go. We spent an extra 20 minutes saying goodbye and then headed back to the Women's Hospital.

It was tough leaving him on his own again but the most important thing was what we learned on the way out: the surgeon had said he was recovering well from his operation, and from what the nurses told us he was taking to the bottle like Miles Davis took to the trumpet.

He was going to get better.

The Bums They Are-A-Changin'

You know you really love someone when you can't wait to change their nappy.

I'd never changed one before. I once helped my mate Craig get into a giant pink one that we'd bought on his stag do, but I was pretty sure that didn't count. Plus he'd not messed himself. We'd probably have been asked to leave Wetherspoon's if that were the case.

I always turned down every opportunity to change nappies before the boys came along. I had a strict rule – I would only clean up the excrement of direct family members. My kids (obviously), my parents (if that day ever comes) and my wife (hopefully nothing to do with the future sexual perversion I mentioned earlier).

Because of this steadfast rule, I refuse to own a dog. My wife is desperate to get one but I know I'll be the one picking up its muck in the rain at 6 a.m. every morning, thus breaking my Family Faeces rule. I also know that my wife will slowly grind me down and one day we will own a dog. I hope I don't write a book about that.

I know some dads pride themselves on never even changing their own kids' nappies but, fellas, if you choose to act like an out-of-touch chauvinist from the Jurassic era, you're really letting the side down. Your wife has pushed a human being through her genitals and is now producing a nutritious beverage with her tits. The least you can do in return is get a bit of shit on your hands.

The first nappy I ever changed felt like a rite of passage. I was supervised by a very patient nurse who shouted encouragement and advice like an amateur boxing coach as Zac ducked and weaved out of my inexperienced grasp. It was one of his first after his operation, which meant that all his insides were now working as planned, lending a party atmosphere to the occasion. If you've never changed a nappy while singing 'Celebration' by Kool & the Gang, you're missing out.

Because Zac was in Alder Hey and Ben had been under the lamp, it didn't feel like we'd been out without our stabilisers yet, but then they finally let Ben move into Rachel's room at the Women's Hospital. Even better, he was out of the incubator and settling into his new hospital-issue bassinet – a tiny cot on wheels. We were so thrilled to have him with us. And scared too – now we had a real-life human being who was completely our responsibility. I tend to always accidentally scuff brand-new shoes, so I was desperate to avoid that with my kids.

I wondered how I'd cope looking after my own child for the first night. The answer was badly.

I couldn't stop watching over him, and when he jolted his head from left to right, planting his head into the side of his cot like an angry Sunday-league centre-half going up for a corner, I went from nought to hysterical in a nanosecond. It obviously didn't bother him in the slightest;

I think he might even have enjoyed it, as he did it again straightaway. I decided to move him away from the side before he completed his hat-trick.

The little sleep we got that night was lighter than Ryvita – every gurgle sounded like he was choking or eating his own head, making me jump out of bed to see him lying there having a great time. He was just seeing what he could do with his brand-new face, like he was checking it out in the shop before putting down a deposit.

The next day, Ben was back under the lamp for the morning so when it was time to get to work I took him out of his baby sunbed for my first solo nappy change. Nobody watching over me. No one to make me extra nervous. Just my son and I. That and a heftily soiled, disposable garment. Independence at last.

I took his nappy off, leaving his protective eye mask on. He immediately pissed all over himself. Then he started crying, because, well, someone was pissing all over him. Wouldn't you?

I decided to take his eye mask off and to show his gratitude he pissed on me and somehow managed to get a load of it all over his own back, defying physics, gravity and common sense in one fell swoop. The guy was clearly a pioneer.

What I learned from that initial dalliance is that the ABSOLUTE golden rule is: BEFORE YOU START A NAPPY CHANGE, FOR GOD'S SAKE MAKE SURE YOU'VE GOT ALL THE BITS YOU NEED.

As a total fuckwit, I can't emphasise this enough. Nothing induces terror more than realising that the cotton wool is out of arm's reach and you're going to have to use your sock.

The second time I did a solo change, I did the other thing you mustn't in a nappy-change situation: I panicked. If you do that you might as well start wearing them yourself. I simply didn't prepare properly. A basic error and frankly, inexcusable for an educated adult. I had most of it ready – the bum cream, the change of clothes, and I even made sure the cotton wool was close at hand with an extra piece to go over his wee man to stop a repeat of last time. I got the scented nappy bag out of the box and opened it in preparation. Let's face it; you don't want to be licking your fingers to get purchase on the bag after you've been wiping your son's over-excitable back door.

But guess which bit I didn't have?

The nappy.

The fucking nappy! The very thing I was there to change.

Have you ever been camping and forgotten the tent? Of course not. Nobody has ever done that because that would be stupid. But my feelings of stupidity were only fleeting because pure and total panic flooded my entire being as I realised the gravity of the situation I was in. I even considered temporarily putting his old one back on while I located the fresh batch but decided that might cause us both severe psychological trauma in later life. In the end I let him wriggle and cry while I walked the five yards to retrieve the new nappy. In the cold light of day it was the obvious thing to do but in the pressure-cooker environment of a botched bum-wash I completely lost it.

At this point I couldn't see how I could ever get to a competent level at this. If this was an online computer game I'd be the guy running against a wall, pressing the wrong buttons while virtuoso American teenagers swore down my headset.

I remember once seeing some Braille on a baby change shelf in a train toilet. I've got total respect for anyone who is blind and lives a full and rewarding life, but if you're able to change the nappy of a wriggling, shitting baby on a high-speed inter-city vehicle WITHOUT THE POWER OF SIGHT then you're not blind – you're a wizard.

That night the previous week's events caught up with me. Dashing between hospitals to see each son – neither critical but neither ready to come home – sucked all the enthusiasm from me. I knew we were the lucky ones. We'd met numerous parents in both hospitals with stories far too tragic to share in detail. That's when the guilt kicked in – why should I be down? What did we have to feel bad about?

Then we were told we could take Ben home tomorrow. He took the news in his stride but we were overjoyed.

Home Alone

After visiting Zac at Alder Hey I made the final journey back up to our room at the Women's Hospital with one of the car seats that had done nothing so far except take up space.

I carried it to our room with such glee that I bashed it into the corner of the lift door, blurting out 'Don't worry, it's empty!' to the doctor who shot me a disapproving look. I decided I should definitely be more careful once Ben was in it but it was the giddiness that caused me to be so clumsy – the last time I was that excited carrying something upstairs was Christmas 1990 when I got my Commodore Amiga computer.

I scooped Ben up and carefully put him into the seat. When you first put your baby into their car seat they pretty much disappear. The buckle was almost the size of his entire face, and despite not being able to convey emotions yet, he looked overwhelmed and not comfortable in the slightest. All I cared about was his safety for the upcoming car journey home. After checking the seat was attached to the base a full seven times, we set off, tackling those pesky speed bumps in a completely different manner to the last time. The car tyres caressed the speed bumps like old lovers as I drove like I was in the slow bike race at sports day.

And then we were home. Well, most of us. Zac was still recovering at Alder Hey as he was now battling with the yellow bastard of jaundice. Still being incomplete made bringing Ben into the family home for the first time less triumphant than I'd imagined. We decided not to put the cards up until we were all together, it just didn't feel right.

After a quick cuppa, my wife set off to visit Zac at Alder Hey and I looked after Ben at home for the first time. It had been easy in the hospital (apart from the odd nappy change), but I'd been surrounded by medical professionals there. I was now walking the parental tightrope without a safety net.

Ben woke up and started crying. *No problem,* I thought. *I'll sort him out a bottle.* But the bottles we'd bought were still in the box and covered in that shrink-wrap stuff that's tighter than a Sumo wrestler's jock strap. So was the steriliser machine, which turned out to be harder to get into than prog rock. I was tempted to just trust that the bottles would be 'box fresh' but after all the breast pump cleaning I'd been through I wasn't taking any chances.

There was going to be a delay before I could feed him so I picked him up and put his face right in front of mine. He opened one eye as I murmured to him, 'It's okay. Your daddy's here. Everything's fine.'

He instantly stopped crying and suddenly seemed content with the world. It felt incredible – connecting with my son on a deep and emotional level. The words I used weren't important to him, but the person who said them was.

This was going to be a doddle.

I put him back in his Moses basket and he started screaming and then threw up on himself.

Like the boys, that thought had been hopelessly premature.

Come Home Baby

Day 3. I had a voicemail from Alder Hey asking me to call them about Zac. My breathing became shallow and the shake of my hands made it nearly impossible to dial the number. The voice on the message had remained neutral so it was hard to read anything from it. Was something wrong? Had his condition worsened?

The answer was none of the above – he was coming home.

This came out of the blue as they'd never put a definite date on his release, just when he was ready. The longer he'd stayed, and the more I'd spoken to other parents on the unit, the fear had grown that it could be months.

But he was coming home.

I offered to pick him up 'because otherwise he'd have to get three buses', but my attempt at humour fell flat down the phone as I could barely string three words together. My voice was quivering and complete sentences weren't within my grasp.

Driving to the hospital I had my iPod synced up and on shuffle. I love it when the music matches up with real life and when 'Come Home Baby' by the Charlatans came on at the lights I had to tell myself to keep it together.

It was a nightmare trying to park at Alder Hey but I didn't get stressed like the other drivers. We were all doing circuits up and down the car park like a giant game of Pac-Man, but as they gurned and grimaced I grinned like a Cheshire cat that had just been made CEO of Elmlea. This was the happiest I'd felt since holding both lads in my arms for the first time.

My son was coming home.

My legs felt lighter walking from the unit door to his room this time, like I'd taken off a pair of heavy boots. He was asleep as I got to his cot so I whispered to him that he was coming home and he started crying, which was unfortunate. I told myself he must have grown fond of the surroundings and the succession of heroes who'd taken care of him.

The nurses gave me some vitamins for him and told me where he was up to with his feeds. Then they asked me what clothes I was taking him home in and I realised I hadn't brought any for him. Deary me. I decided to wait a while to put my Dad of the Year nomination in the post.

There was a delay as the wrong paperwork arrived, and I started to wonder if all these factors would conspire to keep him there another night. I'm not sure I could have gone home to my wife without him. Thankfully the office staff found what they needed before my kidnapping plans were fully formed, and he was wrapped in a set of clothes that someone had donated to the hospital. I was always certain I would never mollycoddle my kids but as I carried Zac out of the unit I looked at all the other incubators and poorly babies and I remembered what he'd been through. It seemed implausible that I wouldn't wrap him in cotton wool until he was in his mid-30s.

The last person I saw as we left the ward was the young mother I'd spoken to on my first visit. We didn't know each other's names but the context of our conversations meant I felt like she was an old friend. She saw I was leaving with Zac and couldn't contain her happiness for us, rubbing him on the head and wishing us the best of luck. I'd love to think I'd be as magnanimous if the roles had been reversed but I'm not sure that'd be the case. I hope they got home in the end.

The sun was shining as we set off from the hospital so I opened Zac's window slightly, recalling those public-service announcements about the dangers of hot cars. Then I remembered they were about dogs so I shut the window again. It suddenly seemed sweltering so I opened the window a tad, feeling like Goldilocks. In the end I put my foot down and made a mental note to buy some car blinds sharpish.

Each set of lights we hit turned red, making me slow down with all the composure of a learner driver who's just stalled on a hill-start. I made conversation all the way, starting off with an apology for forgetting his clothes and then telling him how his twin brother couldn't wait to meet him properly. Halfway home I convinced myself he'd stopped breathing so I pulled into a bus stop to run around and check.

And then we were home. All of us.

I carried him through the front door in his car seat and an unfamiliar feeling washed over me. Is this what it felt like to be relaxed? Ever since they told us about Zac's operation at the 24-week scan we'd both spent every second living in fear, to the point where it quickly just became part of who we were. The apprehension loomed so large and for so long, in the end we forgot it was there. When you get a stone in your shoe sometimes you hobble until you can fix it. Carrying Zac through the front door was tipping gravel out of those heavy boots and putting on a brand-new pair of comfy slippers.

When I got Zac inside, my wife had put Ben on the playmat in our lounge and I got the camera ready to capture their first proper meeting on the outside. We put him and his brother together as I got ready for a classic YouTube click-bait style moment.

'THESE TWINS WERE SEPARATED AT BIRTH. WHAT HAPPENED WHEN THEY WERE REUNITED WILL BLOW YOUR MIND!'

And guess what happened . . .

Nothing. Bugger-all. They just lay there in silence until Ben noisily soiled himself, probably with all the emotion. It was the happiest I'd ever felt.

We spent the rest of the day all huddled together on the sofa, alternating who held each twin. No machines. No tubes. No doctors. Just a young family making up for lost time. We made sure the cards were all up for when Zac arrived home – I don't think he noticed, but you can't be sure. And who knows, maybe one day he'll read this.

That night I looked on as Rachel watched both boys sleeping. Her eyes looked different. Like a light had come back on. As if someone had fixed her.

And for some, what we'd been through temporarily is just normal routine. Those parents I met in the hospital showed a kind of courage and spirit I hadn't seen in the flesh before. A strength beyond what most of us think is possible. Those parents and children are real-life superheroes.

5 Things I Learned from Being a Foursome

1. It's easy to get to midday and realise you've not stopped since 6am but have achieved a grand total of fuck all.

2. I don't care how strong you think you are, nobody is stronger than a baby who doesn't want to get dressed.

3. If something looks like poo and smells like poo, it's poo. If somethings looks like Marmite and smells like Marmite it's probably also poo.

4. Getting your baby to nap is like a game of Snakes and Ladders. One wrong move and you're back to the beginning.

5. Some nappy changes are like Brexit – tonnes of build up, nobody really knows what's going on and there's a horrible mess to clean up afterwards.

Part 3:

The Land
of Nod is
Currently
Closed for
Refurbishment

Tiredness

When we got home I started keeping a diary. Due to exhaustion, I only kept it for less than a week and then gave up. The entries were all, rather aptly, about exhaustion.

Sunday 19th April
Sleep has become the most valuable commodity in our house. We use it to barter with, like cigarettes in prison. When I told my wife she could go back to bed yesterday she looked happier than when I proposed.

I've been in denial all this time. Telling myself and anyone who asks that I'm not too tired at all, thank you very much. Coping really well without sleep, ta for asking. But as I was washing my hands with toothpaste this morning I realised I've been living a lie.

Halfway through a conversation with anyone who isn't my wife I crumple like a papier-mâché armchair. I'm fine for the opening hellos and small talk but as soon as they ask me an important question my brain turns to mush quicker than a frog in a blender. My mouth then joins in on the act and starts slurring random vowels while my face makes a desperate cry for help. The only question that I definitely know the answer to is 'Do you want a cup of coffee, Sam?'

CHRIST, YES I DO.

Monday 20th April

I've drunk that much coffee today I can hear my teeth. Short of a Red Bull enema or chewing on a tube of Berocca I'm not sure what else to do.

This tiredness has crept up on me like a thief at a cashpoint. Sleep is now just an old friend I've lost touch with. We used to be close but we've drifted apart . . .

Dear Sleep,

My oldest, dearest friend. Where have you been?

We had it all, you and I. We never left each other's side – eight hours a night, more at weekends, and even the occasional get-together in the afternoon. Sundays were our special day when we'd overdose on each other's dreamy company until we both felt able to start the new week afresh.

Recently you've started seeming distant and cold. Was it my fling with Coffee that pushed you away?

You know damn well I was only with her because I was missing you. The more you rejected me the more you pushed me into her beany bosom. There wasn't a gulp of espresso I took that I wasn't thinking of you.

Last night you didn't come home at all. Where the hell were you? I needed you today.

I'm sorry. I didn't mean to snap. I'm just so . . . tired. I can't think straight. I know what the end of my wits look like now, in graphic HD detail.

I need you here. You can straighten this all out.

Instead you're out there, cavorting with my friends, the ones without kids. I can't go on Facebook without reading all the disgusting, sordid details. 'Lovely lie-in today.' 'Can't believe I slept for 10 hours straight!'

You used to do that with me. I feel sick just thinking about it.

I took you for granted, I understand that now. I realise we'll never have what we used to but please, please, come back into my life.

All my love and desperation,

Sam (an exhausted new parent) x

Tuesday 21st April

These days I spend more time peeling dried puke from my neck than I do with my eyes shut. As I left the house this morning an elderly gentleman who lives on our street stopped me to ask what day it was. He seemed confused and embarrassed and my heart went out to him. Then I realised I didn't have a clue myself.

I tried to stay confident and reassuring while my brain frantically searched for clues.

'Ooh, hang on. I know this one. Shit. Monday? Have you got any on sport?'

I came clean with him and told him we'd not long had twins and I was – for want of a better word – fucked. It was odd to have a confused senior citizen who's possibly suffering with the early stages of dementia take genuine pity on me with concern for my wellbeing. He suggested I get some sleep, which is like turning up at a fire and recommending water. But he meant well and I hope he's okay. I'll keep an eye out for him from now on. I just hope he doesn't ask me any difficult questions again.

Wednesday 22nd April
Basic decisions elude me. I've spilled three drinks today. One was a milkshake all over my jeans. I'm living in a stain-rich environment at the moment but this one looks rather more dubious than the others.

Thursday 23rd April
I was working in London today appearing on my favourite radio show. Whenever I do this I'm normally excited ON the train but this time I was excited ABOUT the train journey – 2 hours and 21 minutes to sit with my eyes closed and my brain off. It turned out my seat was at a table, normally the Holy Grail of locomotive luxury, but not for a desperate sleep-seeker like me. The train was packed but needs must, so I spent the whole journey

slumping like the Greek economy all over the poor businessman who was crammed in next to me.

Very occasionally (every five minutes) I'd wake myself up when my snoring hit its rhythm, but I'd just wipe the dribble from my chin and repeat the process. Now and again I'd open my eyes to see a lot of people looking at me with disapproving faces but I didn't give two hoots. This was my time and I was gonna sleep.

Friday 24th April

Every night the loan sharks from the Land of Nod keep reminding me that I'm falling behind on my payments and they'll be back tomorrow to break my kneecaps. But until then, I need a triple espresso and a grab bag of Pro-Plus – I have shit to do. Even if I can't quite remember what it is or how to do it.

Bath-Night Blues

One of the things I was really looking forward to when the kids got home was bath night.

Not for me, you understand – I'm strictly a shower man. I can't think of anything worse than sitting in your own filth for half an hour while the water gets cold and the bubbles disappear to remind you that no matter how hard you try, love handles don't tuck in. And anyway, it's impossible to look as svelte as you do in that generous mirror in the work lift when you're stewing in the tub, struggling to reach your arm around your jelly belly to give your bum crack a good flannel rub.

But a kid's bathtime is like a trip to Alton Towers without the queues. They love it. Splashing about, playing with rubber ducks. I couldn't wait to see their little faces.

The first time we put our two in the water we treated it like a red letter day. We posed for photos, sang some songs, and then they screamed like Al Pacino at the end of *The Godfather Part III*. I'm sure next door thought we were waterboarding terror suspects.

The whimpering started when I took their sleepsuits off. It went up a notch when I took them out of their nappies. *No bother*, I thought. *As soon as that nice warm water hits their skin they'll be purring like pussycats.*

That was a misjudgement of the highest order. This is how I learned that little babies (or our two in any case) would rather stink like a yak's armpits than get a good wash. As it happened, the tiny crying as I got them ready was just the quiet verse in the baby emo-rock classic they were improvising together. The Slipknot-influenced chorus kicked in as they touched the water.

And then the wriggling started. Zac went at it like the bath was Greenwich Village, NYC circa 1984 and he was a breakdancing champion. With Ben it was all about the legs – kicking viciously but with enough rhythm to send him spinning round in my wife's hands like an out-of-control Benidorm pedalo. It was lovely to see them developing their own personalities.

Their twitching forced their bodies out of the water and into the cold air, which made them scream even more, forcing them to twist even harder. I made the executive decision to end the bath at that point, like a boxing referee calling a match, so we pulled them both out of the water. Just as the scene was starting to resemble the cover shot of *Pole Fishing* monthly, the screaming went to a level I'd never experienced before, as if Marilyn Manson had been unfortunate enough to get his tackle stuck in some farming equipment.

Two nights later we tried again. This one started off so promisingly – no cries when I removed the sleepsuits and only a mild frown when nappies were taken off. Then we slowly lowered them into the perfectly monitored bathwater like you might carefully dunk a wafer biscuit into your cuppa, and still no tears. In fact, Ben pulled one of those grimace-cum-smirk faces that babies seem to be keen on. We dunked them a little deeper until both lads had their legs fully submerged.

They looked at each other and then at us, then both grumbled a low-end murmur that seemed to suggest they were enjoying this against their better instincts.

'I wasn't expecting to enjoy this, Zachary, but I have to be honest and say that it's not bad. Not too shabby at all . . .'

I got over-confident at this point and dripped about a thimbleful of water onto Zac's shoulders. He was quick to let me know this was a mistake.

The transition from total bliss to sheer terror was almost immediate. There was a brief but beautiful moment when their synchronised screaming connected in a divine harmony. But it was a short-lived moment of respite in an otherwise miserable 10 minutes, like someone complimenting your shoes in the middle of a savage street beating. We went back to using wet wipes for the next week or so. *Maybe they're just shower men like their father*, we thought.

Nappy Flap Flop

I was in a vicious cycle. Because I was tired, I was clumsy. Because I was clumsy I dropped things. Because I dropped things, I woke the babies. Because I woke the babies I was tired.

Most of my days played out like this:

5.45 a.m.
F**k this. Snooze button. SNOOZE BUTTON. Another seven minutes will sort me out.

5.47 a.m.
Well that was a blissful 120 seconds. Best get up and get them downstairs. That screaming from the next room is like being at the dentist.

5.52 a.m.
Is that my snoozed alarm going off upstairs? Listen to the bloody thing. It's mocking me. Desperate for a brew here.

drops kettle on foot

BASTARD! Christ, I hope it's not broken. The kettle that is, not arsed about my foot. Need coffee badly.

6.40 a.m.
I feel fine now. I really love being up at this time anyway. The lads are happy and smiling. Life is perfect.

9.35 a.m.

CHRIST. I'd donate a body part to go back to bed. Not a leg or anything like that. Just a toe. My little toe. Doesn't do much anyway. Definitely cut my toe off for another two hours. Maybe I'd bargain for three hours actually. It is my toe after all.

10.40 a.m.

I WOULD HACK MY OWN ARM OFF WITH A RUSTY SAW FOR 20 MINUTES WITH MY EYES SHUT.

11.05 a.m.

Need more coffee. God, I need coffee. I'm definitely addicted. If they made coffee illegal I'd probably get involved in all sorts of petty crime.

11.20 a.m.

Wow. I'm buzzing now. Another large cup, methinks.

12.05 p.m.

Jesus God Almighty, I feel fantastic! Think I'll have a go at that grouting in the kitchen when the lads have a nap. Best put the kettle on again.

1.15 p.m.

Think I overdid the coffee. Feel weird now. Can't think straight. Teeth are grinding. Face feels like it's vibrating.

2.20 p.m.

Uuuuuuuuuhhhhhhhhm?

4.05 p.m.
Feeling mildly depressed. Must be a comedown from all the coffee. Need something else to keep me going though. Isn't there a can of that mad energy drink in the fridge?

4.10 p.m.
How is this stuff available over the counter, it's frigging nuclear! No wonder kids are all stabbing each other drinking this shit every day.

5.15 p.m.
Flagging again. Need chocolate now. Or cake. Just mainline sugar into my eyes, please. Help me?

6 p.m.
Nearly there. Or am I hallucinating? Why are new parents the ones who are sleep-deprived? We need sleep more than anyone! It's not fair. Feel like weeping. Jesus, pull yourself together, you pathetic excuse for a man.

6.35 p.m.
All those lie-ins I used to have, I never appreciated them at the time. What a waste.

7.05 p.m.
Lads are in bed. Should definitely go to bed myself. Can still feel the effects of that energy drink though. Plus I need some 'me' time now. Where's that bottle of wine?

After that I'd stay up till midnight watching bad telly and then repeat the process the following day, which obviously affected my judgement over time.

Then something happened when the boys were about three months that I'll never forget. And it was all my fault.

I can't believe I did it. I honestly never thought I'd be so stupid as to let this happen. But it happened. Oh boy, did it happen.

It was avoidable, so completely escapable. I need to try to look forward – it's in the past now. But that's impossible – it's embedded on my brain like a cheap tattoo. I promise you, I'll never be the same again.

Most parents will remember the first time their child flashed them a smile, or babbled their first proper word. I'm sure I'll remember those things in time but I also know I'll never forget the day when I didn't pull the flaps out of the nappy properly.

How could I have been so stupid? I'd changed loads of nappies by this point and despite still being more hapless than Captain Hook in a Tiddlywinks tournament I'd at least avoided any liquid-based catastrophes.

But not on this particular day. My God. What a mess.

I'd received a warning a few nights before when I managed to remember at the last minute that I hadn't pulled the flaps out of Ben's nappy after I'd put him down in his basket. I was on the verge of drifting off to sleep when the thought hit me like a Frisbee in the ear and I bolted upright in bed. My wife asked me what was wrong, probably suspecting I'd had an accident myself.

'Flaps!' I calmly declared as I went over to the Moses baskets. It was my eureka moment.

But on this occasion I wasn't so lucky. And I'll never un-see what I saw.

I'd changed both nappies in record time for me – 12 minutes, 34 seconds. A small wave of unnecessary smugness washed over me for the next few hours until I noticed that Ben was starting to smell like a sweet-shop bin. I picked him up and he started to cry. So I felt the back of his legs and they were wetter than Wet Wet Wet on a log flume.

That's when I started to replay the previous nappy change in my head, piecing events together. I started to hope it was just the sheer force of his movement that had caused the leak – this would absolve me of blame. But I couldn't remember the details of the last change and I feared I'd absentmindedly cut corners which would leave me completely culpable.

I opened his sleepsuit like a nervous teenager getting their GCSE results. It turned out I'll be resitting all of them.

My son had turned into a slurry truck with legs. Even his tiny face that was still finding its way in the world managed to flash me a look that said, *You did this, you stupid man. I promise you this – do it just one more time and I'll have you in a nursing home before you're 50.*

The philosopher George Santayana said, 'Those who do not remember the past are condemned to repeat it.' Scholars have endlessly debated over whether he was referring to political hierarchical manoeuvrings or merely commentating on the increasingly obsolete religious structures of the day.

I'm pretty sure he was talking about an open-flap shit leak in his son's nappy.

Arguments by Proxy

When kids arrive, tensions run high. It's the happiest time of your life (so you're told) and you should apparently 'enjoy every moment', so why do you feel like you want to scream? Well, let's review the evidence. If you are a new parent or a parent of young children, please tick the relevant box if:

- ☐ Your sleep has been cut in half (if you're lucky)
- ☐ Your free time has evaporated
- ☐ The taste of a still-warm cuppa is now a distant memory
- ☐ You've left the house with numerous stains on your trousers
- ☐ The most relaxing thing you can do is a hard day at work

In fact if this was a workplace you'd be stood on a picket line demanding better conditions. Not that you'd have the time to strike of course, mainly because you've got 400 metric tonnes of washing to get through before bedtime, and that's not before you've scraped the eclectic congregation of unidentifiable stains off the skirting board that've been crusting over since the previous tax year. Your house is now impossible to actually clean. You can move things around and put them in different rooms but your house will remain a shithole.

But there is no option but to carry on in the face of testing circumstances.

Kids do their part by seeming to unconsciously know when they've pushed you right to the edge and are able to bring you back with an act of unspeakable cuteness. There must be a mechanism programmed into human DNA that allows toddlers to recognise when they need to rescue the situation.

'Mission control, this is your subconscious calling. We have observed that you poured your entire drink over your mother's iPad after spending the day being highly uncooperative. We recommend that now would be an effective moment to deploy your attempt at a brand new word. Any word – with a smile. Just remember, make it cute. Over and out.'

'D-d-d-DOOR!'

Aww.

I felt completely lost and almost dizzy with stress one day when one of our boys took it upon himself to crawl over to the TV and start waving at the contestants on *The Chase*. The impending doom melted like ice.

Love really is the answer.

So despite the fact that life is clearly 'very good' it can sometimes feel 'quite bad'. I'm pretty sure anyone who coasts through parenthood without ever questioning themselves or wishing they could just have a week off from it all isn't actually a real parent. They're probably genetically engineered in a lab by the government and would be the most boring people in the world. Can you imagine their tedious stories?

'Last week, we put him down for his nap and he slept for almost THREE hours.'

'Three hours, huh? That's beautiful, because yesterday I got ACTUAL SHIT IN MY EYE.'

'. . .'

All this adds a certain frisson to your relationship with your partner (and to any single parents reading, I doff my cap to you. You are legends).

The first couple of years of being parents together takes your relationship by the scruff of the neck and forces it onto an assault course at dawn. A misplaced inflection on a word can cause a squabble. Leaving clean washing in the wrong pile is a potential flare-up. And accidentally putting a dirty nappy in the washing machine will definitely throw your marriage onto the rocks.

When it comes to the relationship with your other half, the most simple and memorable piece of parenting advice I received came from comedian Rob Rouse. He told me that no matter how tired you think YOU are, your partner will be feeling EXACTLY THE SAME.

So many times I got myself wrapped up in my own exhaustion, forgetting that Rachel would have been feeling just as knackered as I was – probably even more so.

Yet, there's something about the early years of parenthood and the sleep deprivation that comes with it that at times turns you into an unreasonable monster. Logic and empathy seem to disappear from your skill set temporarily. I remember one morning when it was my wife's turn to do the early feed and the boys didn't wake up till 8 a.m. I should have been pleased for her but I was absolutely fuming.

It just wasn't fair.

We didn't have any full-on arguments but we're probably lucky in that we tend to avoid those. Often my wife will resort to pulling my trousers down if an exchange is beginning to get a little heated, thus winning and losing any argument simultaneously. (Although I did learn that joking to your wife that you really appreciate her 'doing her 49% share of everything' is definitely not funny in the slightest.)

What we did do in those early days was have a tonne of by-proxy digs at each other, by talking to the boys about each other. The jibes would start off as a bit of fun but tended to escalate out of control.

'I thought Daddy would have done that washing-up by now.'

'Well, it's okay for Mummy to say that as she had a lie-in this morning.'

'But Daddy isn't pumping out fresh milk from his boobies, is he? Even though he looks like he's got all the relevant equipment.'

'That's a bit rich coming from Mummy, isn't it?'

'Is Daddy calling Mummy fat? Because Mummy will wait till Daddy's asleep and cut his silly little balls off.'

'As long as Mummy doesn't wake Daddy up that doesn't actually sound too bad.'

I've spoken to people who try for a baby to 'save' their relationship. I'm sure there are occasions when it's been successful, but I can't think of anything worse for a failing marriage than to throw a newborn baby into the mix. You'd have more chance of stopping a boat from capsizing by chucking half a dozen rabid baboons on board. I was always able to rescue any cross words between Rachel and me with what I learned to be the most romantic gesture of them all: no need for trips to Paris or expensive jewellery, just turn to your partner and whisper, 'Babe – I'll have the baby monitor on my side of the bed tonight if you like.'

What a smoothie.

The Great Escape (from our House)

Day 21. We'd spent so long cooped up in the house since we got back from hospital that it was starting to feel like prison, although I presume prisons smell better. It was time for our first day out (I use the word 'day' even though we were only out for less than an hour. It just took all day to get ready).

First thing to negotiate was the pram. It was time to test this second hand thing we'd bought to see if it all worked properly. I'm sure it's a piece of cake if you know what you're doing. If you haven't got a clue it's a massive Rubik's Cube you're scared to break. I loved Transformers as a kid but I'm permanently scarred from snapping Megatron's leg off one Christmas with a hapless transform attempt. I spent the next few weeks trying to convince my mates that he was only supposed to have one leg but they weren't buying it. And when my parents wouldn't buy me a new one and his recently detached limb disappeared, I ended up breaking the leg off my Mr. T figure and surgically connecting it to poor old Megatron with some chewed-up Hubba Bubba. The results were less than satisfying, and I don't think Mr. T was too impressed with my Dr Frankenstein-style solution either.

So I was being very careful when pushing and pulling the various bits of the pram, trying to make them click into place. There are so many accessories that it's difficult to know which is which, and at times I felt like I was on *The Cube* trying to complete a task. At one point I had the carrycot clipped on sideways which made it look more like an incredibly middle-class wheelbarrow. After a few botched attempts and even more swearwords, I eventually got it up and running.

Rachel and I fed both the lads, changed and dressed them into their first going-out clothes. They looked super cute so I grabbed the camera just in time to see Ben puke all over himself. I picked him up to try to minimise the damage and he perfectly aimed his second wave right down my T-shirt. I took Ben into the next room, and through the doorway behind me heard Zac make a belch noise that sounded like a disgruntled frog watching his team lose. As burps go, this one sounded wetter than a Volvic staff away day to the swimming baths.

I dashed back in but Zac hadn't actually puked. It had been that rarest and most beautiful of occurrences: a clean burp. The excitement and misplaced pride took over my better judgement and I stooped down to kiss him on the cheek with a slightly patronising 'Well done, son'. As my lips touched his cheeks he vomited with the force of an angry power shower. His timing was impeccable because he managed to coat me, Ben and himself in almost equal amounts of his second hand milk. It looked like the Stay Puft Marshmallow Man had exploded in our living room.

Then he started to cry. As he inhaled between bawls he got a rogue piece of regurgitated milk wedged in his nostril, which made him cry even more. This made Ben cry too for some reason, I presume in a loyal act of brotherly empathy. I considered joining them for a split second before remembering that I'm an adult and this is all part of the rich experience of parenthood. Anyway, how would we appreciate the highs without the lows? I can't even begin to enjoy a picnic unless I've first been stung in the eye by a wasp.

We changed them into new going-out outfits and got them into the pram. I felt a rumbling in Zac but didn't know which way it was heading. It turned out the rumble didn't know either and decided to hedge its bets and go both ways for a classic puke/trump Dirty Double©. It wasn't comparable to the first phase but, like an earthquake's aftershock, there was still considerable damage, although on this occasion mainly to my emotional wellbeing. We changed them once again, this time into scruffy sleepsuits as there were no more going-out clothes left that we wanted instantly ruining.

We were making progress slower than an earthworm who's just got into homebrewing. But at least it was progress. Sort of.

Pram assembled? Check!

Babies in pram? Check!

Time to leave the house, finally! But the pram was too big for our front door so we had to dismantle the whole thing and reassemble it outside. The day was slipping away from us like a bar of cheap soap in a campsite shower block, but at least we were outside now. Walking down our street pushing our lads for the first time felt liberating. A neighbour stopped us and said he didn't realise we'd had a baby. 'We've had two!' we both chimed, in sugary-sweet unison.

But aside from that pleasant interlude, I was suddenly very aware of every possible threat to my sons, and of my new role as protector. I was swatting away flies and nearly swung a punch at a poor bee that buzzed through our periphery. Then there were the dogs.

I'm petrified of dogs, or at least I used to be. I heard some loud, aggressive barking behind us and instead of me freezing up and a bit of wee coming out like normal, I slowly turned round to confront this wild beast. I could barely believe what I was doing but I managed to stand my ground directly in between this rabid monster and my family (think George McFly finally fronting up to Biff in *Back to the Future*). I looked this thing dead in the eye and with the body language of a grizzly bear played by Joe Pesci I mouthed the words *DON'T YOU COME A STEP CLOSER, BUDDY BOY*, until it gave up and trotted off. I can't stand Jack Russells.

Crossing the road hasn't felt like a challenge since I was eight, but with this pram in front of me I was now playing a real life game of Frogger. I naively thought that all the traffic would stop when they saw a double pram trying to get across the road but they seemed to speed up if anything, the bastards.

But finally we were there! We'd made it to the park. The big glorious green land of freedom. Except all our time was taken up by strangers stopping us to coo over the boys. It was lovely the first 12 times but then it did start to drag a bit.

'Ooooh, how much did they weigh?' (Women love asking that question about babies but are never as keen to share their own stats with the world.)

And then it was time to come home.

On the way back we found ourselves in a Mexican stand-off with another pram on a thin piece of pavement. I was about to move back (why don't prams have wing mirrors FFS?) but they quickly moved out of the way. I felt like the big truck in Stephen King's *Duel*. I thought, *I could throw my weight around with this pram* . . .

It was getting dark by the time we got back home. We felt like we'd circumnavigated the Gobi Desert.

We'd been out of the house for 47 minutes.

Tandem-Feed Fiasco

Despite the odd quarrel, by the time the boys were a month or so old we were settling into a decent routine at home. But a big problem we had was that it took ages to feed each baby, and by that I mean it was quicker to read the entire terms and conditions for iTunes than feed both twins separately. But that's what we did for ages, one after the other.

My wife kept talking about this mystical 'tandem feed' that we should employ but I kept brushing it off like she was suggesting we start a new box set that required total concentration.

'Yeah, love. Deffo up for having another go at *Game of Thrones* tomorrow. Let's finish *Mad Men* first though, eh?'

I'm a creature of habit and don't like change, even if that change is clearly an improvement. If I had owned a mill in 1764 I'd have told you to shove your spinning jenny and instead ordered more smallpox-riddled peasants for my workforce. The thought of trying to feed and burp the boys at the same time filled me with dread, as the only multitasking I can handle involves sitting on the toilet with the Sunday papers (I'm not proud of this).

But I was a grown man and a father now, and by God I was going to give it a go, so I put Ben on my lap and reached for Zac. By the time I'd got Zac into position (about 1.3 seconds) Ben had wriggled away like Harrison Ford in

The Fugitive. Being still so young the boys couldn't wriggle especially well: they'd lead with their faces, meaning they'd struggle to get much choice over their destination. Ben ended up face down on the sofa for a split second, which didn't help anyone.

So I grabbed Ben and while I did this Zac opted for the same pointless escape route. It felt like an impromptu game of Whac-A-Mole without a mallet.

I knew I needed to pin them down to maintain some form of order but I was still very aware that they were little babies and the last thing I wanted to do was accidentally hurt them. When I first picked Zac up at the hospital I did the classic I'm-a-new-dad-so-I'm-holding-my-baby-like-it's-live-explosives routine, and the midwife said 'Don't worry. You can't break him.' I remember thinking that she hadn't seen just how clumsy I could be (I once trod dog muck into my mum's new carpet, kicked over a pint of Tizer and blew the fuse for the living room in the space of eight seconds).

So I put my hand on Zac's chest and tried to manoeuvre Ben back into position. I was starting to feel like a pathetic supply teacher who'd lost control of his class at this point, so I decided to hurry things along and try to get the bottles in. I grabbed one with each hand and aimed for the boys' mouths, getting Ben in the ear and Zac in the stomach somehow. I had another go, feeling like a nervous skier. This time I hit the jackpot and both teats landed in their mouths. I wanted to wave to the crowd like a golfer who'd just putted a birdie but I didn't have a free hand and there was no crowd. So I didn't.

At first Ben decided he'd forgotten how to feed and was biting at the teat like it was corn on the cob at his end-of-diet celebratory barbecue. But once I readjusted there was a blissful moment as both boys instantly stopped wriggling and started gurgling with sheer pleasure. For a short time they perfectly took it in turns to coo, and if I closed my eyes I felt like the umpire at the cutest tennis match of all time (I realise that tennis umpires probably keep their eyes open during rallies).

After five minutes of total calm it was time to burp them so I took out their bottles. The beautiful silence vanished – quicker than my credibility when I'd mistakenly come dressed as Austin Powers to a party that definitely wasn't fancy dress – and was replaced by a noisy kind of chaos I hadn't experienced up to this point, with both boys thrashing their limbs about and screaming like it was an Iron Maiden audition.

My customary panic kicked into overdrive and all decision-making skills left the room.

I grabbed Ben and lifted him over my shoulder but as I did so he puked right down my front. Zac had started to do that baby cry that morphs into an angry cough so I quickly grabbed him and tried to coax a burp out, but he was having none of it. I felt like I was suddenly afflicted by an aggressive form of tinnitus in my right ear so I put him down and reached for his dummy but it was just out of reach. Like Frodo desperately scrambling for the Ring on Mount Doom I just managed to grab it, as this situation was far more perilous than a millennia of dark rule over the Shire.

Putting their dummies in had an amazing effect, like plugging a hole in the bath of madness. I hadn't burped them properly but it was proving impossible, so after getting my breath back I put their bottles back in. Risky business.

They took the next portion of their bottles like it was night one on their first lads' holiday to Magaluf, but they wouldn't stop squirming out of position. Ben was moving his head from side to side like a bad Stevie Wonder imper-sonator and Zac kept trying to break into a rendition of the Cossack dance by kicking his legs all over the shop. But as burping them had proved more tricky than plate-spinning, I decided to go right through to the end of the feed without any more attempts. This was to prove my ultimate undoing.

As they finished the last of their formula I continued the lads' holiday theme by putting both bottles on my head and shouting 'Waaaaaaay!' like a proper tit. They also continued this theme by simultaneously ejecting a week's supply of vomit all over me.

It was an awful scene. I hadn't had this much puke on me since the night I discovered how to make Cheeky Vimto – both lads just let rip and covered me like I was in the gunk tank on *Fun House*.

I didn't know what to do next – should I move them away from the river of filth? Should I move one and try to clean the other with the sleeve of my T-shirt? Should I be a man about this or should I just panic and shout for my wife?

'BABE! GET IN HERE! PLEASE! WE'VE GOT A SITUATION!'

The Curious Case of Benjamin's Belly Button (and Other Stories)

I'm not someone who claims to know everything. Far from it, my knowledge has more gaps than Shane MacGowan's teeth. For instance, I never knew that 1,367 was a prime number or that camel's milk doesn't curdle, and these are basic, simple facts that most people know from birth. Right, guys?

But one thing I'm sure nobody realises until they have a baby themselves is that certain aspects of them are more distasteful than a rat in a restaurant who's decked in double denim and belching the national anthem.

We don't tend to focus on the truly gross parts of having a baby. All the attention is – quite correctly – on the incredible feelings of connection and bond to your newborn, or the overwhelming sense of protection you have towards your baby.

Nobody pulls you aside and says, 'See that baby? They'll make you happier than you ever thought possible. Now, see those neck folds? Cheesy as fuck, mate. Worse than their arse. Every time you put your fingers in there you'll be sick in your own mouth.'

The first time I washed my boys' necks it was like rummaging under my nan's old settee. Bits of fluff, congealed formula and fragments of puke all coalesced to create a matter so foul that it stank like a milkshake that had sat in the sun for a week. And the folds were huge, like dungaree pockets. I half expected to find my house keys in there.

I could have done with somebody to warn me about that.

'And while you're here, I should tell you that they're gonna dribble SO much that some days you'll feel like a batallion of slugs has danced the *Macarena* all over your trousers.'

That would've been good advice too.

'Oh, and sometimes their shite is green.'

Okay, you can stop now. Hang on – green?

'Green, yellow, orange . . . Forget the Bristol Stool Chart, you'll need the Dulux colour chart to know what's going on.'

Perhaps my most alarming discovery of all in those early days is that sometimes a baby's belly button doesn't drop off immediately. I never knew this.

I'm not a prude, and I don't tend to get squeamish, but that scabby piece of Ribena crust is enough to turn your stomach. Especially when you're changing the baby's nappy and his belly button pops its head down just to see what's going on, like a hyperactive puppy when the doorbell rings.

'Hey, guys! What's happening down here? Something's happening! Can I get involved? Please let me get involved!'

I've documented my problems with nappy changing already and this didn't help one bit. In the hospital I remember staring at this putrid string of aubergine for the first time and I'm not going to lie, I thought it was his willy. While totally horrified at the colour and its general demeanour, part of me was jealous of the size. Then I realised it was pegged down, which was weird. So I quickly checked the other babies on the Special Care ward and they all had them too, even the girls. Then I noticed it was hanging off his belly-button area, which should have made things obvious from the beginning really.

Zac's fell off while he was still in hospital. Ben's hung on for three weeks like an unwanted party guest at your house. In the end we turned the music off and started yawning until it got the hint and phoned a taxi.

When it fell off it was the middle of the night and my sleep-deprived stupor made me think it was wriggling away like some kind of fugitive louse. I was half tempted to go and grab a glass and envelope like you do with a spider. When sanity prevailed and I saw it was just a tiny piece of gristle, I actually considered putting it in the memory box we've been putting together for the boys, but quickly realised that would be fairly gruesome. Especially if you opened the box years later and it wasn't there. I can hear the creepy horror music just thinking about it.

If I ever meet whoever designed the prototype for newborn babies I'd compliment them on the standard design and most of the added features, but I'd definitely suggest something a bit more user-friendly in place of these disgusting belly button things. Maybe a USB port or something. And don't get me started on the fact that sometimes babies forget to breathe for up to 10 seconds. TEN SECONDS. Whoever came up with that needs a slap.

Why, Son? Why?

With this book, I wanted to capture my emotional journey into parenthood. But let's face it, a lot of that journey is dealing with bodily functions. Your entire life changes when you have kids. The most beautiful phrase in the English language used to be *I love you* – now it's *puke-free burp*.

At the other end of the spectrum I had a new and terrible three-word phrase which was up there with *rail replacement bus* and *his was bigger. He hasn't pooed.* Although it's all about context – if you say this yourself after a nappy change then it means you dodged a shitty bullet and it's party time. If your wife casually throws it your way as she heads off to bed before you take the reins of the late feed then you know you're in for a grisly affair.

On one occasion when the boys were just over three months old, Ben's nappy was appalling, a 10-wiper. To his credit he lay still and let me clean his rump with minimum fuss, like a Roman emperor being attended to by his minions.

Next came Zac and that's where business really picked up. Some nappy changes turn into a show, and this was our Live Aid. It began as I picked him up and noticed the smell – an unsettling combination of burnt Quavers and treacle pudding. I felt sick and hungry at the same time, like just after you've eaten a McDonald's.

I opened his nappy and it was clean. Suspiciously clean. Almost *too* clean. Heavy, but none of the brown stuff. If I was quick I knew I'd get away with it and the wife would have to mop up the consequences at 3 a.m. The perfect scenario.

I whipped his old nappy away like that tablecloth trick that leaves the plates and cutlery in place, because he had a look on his face that told me a storm was brewing.

I gave his bum a cursory wipe and reached for the new nappy. That's when I heard it. He let out a caustic grunt that belonged in the Olympic clean and jerk, which told me I had a split second to get the new nappy in place. Hitting the panic button I stupidly dropped the new nappy on top of the old nappy, causing the adhesive bits to stick together like a fecal daisy chain, and as I fumbled for another new one he began to trump.

I've heard a million different farts in my time but never one like this. It was majestic, celebratory, as if he were signalling the triumphant return home of his troops from a victorious battle. I also felt the full force of its gust on my hand – it could have dried towels.

Then the trump played its final note and for the briefest of moments there was silence. The pure and total kind I get at some of my gigs. He looked me dead in the eye and took a deep breath as a frown more gloomy than a Morrissey B-side descended upon his face.

And then it came. A river of Marmite. And it kept on coming. There's not much you can do while it's in progress, you just have to let it happen, like an ice hockey ref waiting for a fight to finish before he steps in.

But it didn't end. It was relentless, like a Bruce Springsteen gig or a Welsh town name. I managed to keep my panic at bay but only until we began to run out of changing mat – he was covering the whole thing like he was playing a dirty game of Risk. I wanted to move him away from the danger zone but that was impossible – he WAS the danger zone. He was now doing an uncanny impression of a manic arcade penny-pusher machine, kicking his legs back and forth, pushing it off the mat and onto the carpet. I noticed he'd got some on his foot, which he then smeared onto his leg, and which somehow ended up on my hand and then my T-shirt.

The whole horrible scene resembled an explosion in a Nutella factory. I didn't know what to do or where to turn. I just sat there, filled with panic, covered in my son's excrement, and wondered, *Is this it? Is this what parenthood is all about? Poo?*

Then he smiled.

And then, for the first time ever, he giggled.

Instantly, none of the previous 10 minutes mattered. In fact, nothing else in the history of the world mattered. Just a baby smiling at his father and his father welling up with joy.

I wiped a tear from my face and in doing so smudged a tiny globule of poo across my cheek. I tried to tell myself it didn't matter, but in my book faces and poo should never meet. They shouldn't even exchange pleasantries, never mind get up close and personal with each other.

I didn't learn anything practical that day but I did acknowledge that this was the perfect metaphor for parent-hood: tears of joy streaming down your face, mixed with a loving side order of your own child's shit.

Baby Fat

I always thought the phrase 'baby fat' referred to the baby, not the parent. But in keeping with my boys' piling on the pounds, I too started to gain weight like an old sleeping bag left out in the rain.

Some people say they have a complicated relationship with food. I don't. My relationship with food is very simple. I fucking love it. And the more unhealthy and stodgy it is, the more I want to put it in my face. I enjoy exercise, but I like food more.

It seemed like a warning when I sat on the toilet and it creaked. That shouldn't happen. It was time to do my first exercise since the twins were born. (Such was my performance you'd think I'd spent that entire time living in a crack den.)

People talk about fitness being important, but who has the time as a new parent?

I once heard someone on the radio say, 'When my baby was born I was back in the gym that weekend and, you know, it just gave me so much energy to be able to be an all-round great mother.'

Do me a favour – take those toned glutes and squat-thrusts and get the frig off my radio will you? We neither want or need to hear this. The pressure on new mums to lose the baby weight straightaway is stifling enough in modern Western society. Magazines champion the latest vacuous celebrity who's popped out a sprog, plastering their front cover with airbrushed pictures of their chiselled six-pack a fortnight after the baby's arrived, turning the rest of us into guilt-filled slob merchants as we queue for our party-box of Maltesers. This never happened years ago, did it? Prehistoric females were never forced to stare at cave paintings of brand-new cave-mums looking super ripped in their skimpy loincloths, making them feel fat and inferior.

But if it makes you feel any better, new mums, my diet had been so bad since the babies arrived that I'm sure I could taste cholesterol in a burp some days. I tried to put on a pair of my jeans and nearly had to call the fire brigade when my arse cheek got stuck.

On more than one bleary-eyed morning, breakfast had consisted of four chocolate digestives, two packets of crisps and a cup of coffee. The other day this was followed by a large piece of cheesecake that was just sitting there, giving me the eye.

I then went back into the kitchen for a 'browse'. Big mistake. When I'm running on empty, a 'browse' translates as: *searching for additional foodstuffs that are high in sugar and low in health benefits to insert into my face.* Before I knew it I was throwing biscuit after biscuit into my mush. With every bite came added inner turmoil. I felt like Gollum with an eating disorder.

ME: You deserve this biscuit. You've hardly slept.
CONSCIENCE: But think of the calories! You're getting fat and it's not even Christmas!

ME: Ignore him. You need the sugar. It'll give
               you the energy you need.
CONSCIENCE: You've already had a vat of coffee. How
               much more false energy do you need?
ME: Just keep shovelling those things into your
               mouth. Mmm, enjoy the taste. You've
               earned this little treat.
CONSCIENCE: Little treat?! You've eaten two-thirds of the
               packet already, you fat bastard!

I was insisting to myself that each one would be the last.
I could only believe it with confidence as I scrunched up
the empty packet to put in the bin.

If you can survive on fruit and falafel when you're knackered then you're clearly a better human than me. I also
doubt we'll ever be close friends. I'm more likely to be
seen standing in the kitchen in my underpants, crying to
myself while shovelling Ben & Jerry's ice cream into my
mouth. Straight from the tub. And if there's no clean spoon
I'll use a pen.

And if that mental image doesn't put you off your dinner
then you're probably very similar to me.

I knew I needed to do something – I was so lethargic some
days that I felt more broken than a vase that's been thrown
down the stairs. So I went along to my old regular game
of five-a-side football. The first 10 minutes were okay – I
paced myself and didn't do anything stupid like run or
sweat. Then I got a lucky bounce that spooned off my
shin and dribbled into the net, which gave me something

that nobody lacking in skill and fitness should ever have
– confidence.

Now I was shouting for the ball and trying to get involved
in tactics, while the other players seemed to look at me
thinking, *Why is this fat Sam-lookalike shouting at us?*

Then I got myself into a situation. I called for the ball
and our player booted it right down the wing, causing me
to jog for it. I quickly realised I should start moving a bit
quicker if I wanted to stand any chance of getting to it, so I
started to motor through the gears (I use the word 'motor'
in the loosest possible sense: I was accelerating with all
the vigour of a dilapidated canal barge).

Finally I reached my full speed. I knew this because
I could feel my tits bouncing up and down. Yes – tits.
Not man-boobs, or 'moobs' if you're hip. Just good old-
fashioned boobs, bouncing up and down in time with my
hapless and heavy strides. Where the hell had they sprung
from? I wasn't even aware I had cleavage until it started
jiggling about beneath my numerous chins.

I felt like Pamela Anderson at the beginning of *Baywatch*,
jugs bouncing in slow motion. Was I too old for a starter
bra?

Running felt weird, an out-of-body experience. My whole
frame felt bigger and harder to control, like trying to drive
your dad's work van when you're used to a Fiesta. It was
no surprise that my opponent got to the ball before me
but now I had to figure out how to slow down and stop.

I was tempted to just keep running in the same direction and join in with the game on the adjacent pitch, but
thankfully sanity prevailed and I managed to use the treacle

that I'd been running in to my advantage. Turning with all the grace of a capsizing ocean liner I somehow slammed on the brakes and started to spin back towards the game. The only thing missing was that beeping noise that lorries make when they reverse.

And that was me done. I had nothing left to give after my failed attack. My legs felt heavier than a Black Sabbath chorus but there were still 45 minutes to play, and there's only so many times you can tie your shoelaces while trying not to cry. Add to that a textbook case of 'jogger's nipple', which gave me some insight into the pain women must suffer when breastfeeding. The chafing was as relentless and irritating as those automated PPI phone calls.

I knew I'd nearly made it to the end when the next group started lining up on the touchline – about 30 teenage lads who started cheering good tackles and nice cross-field passes, so obviously we all tried to raise our game due to the sudden 'big-match atmosphere'.

Then something mad happened. I got the ball in my own area. Due to my baldness the lads on the touchline started calling me Robben, after the lightning-quick Dutch dynamo Arjen Robben, and this name seemed to seep into my inner being as I began uncharacteristically jinking and japing through our midfield.

The cheering got louder with every tackle I rode, and – insanely – no one could get near my dazzling run. After it seemed like I'd beaten all of the other team's players twice, I was suddenly one-on-one with their keeper, but was starting to lose my balance away from goal. My new fans held their breath as their idol managed to shift his body weight and defy the laws of physics to scoop the ball gracefully over the advancing keeper and into the empty net.

Fucking pandemonium.

The crowd went ballistic and I sank to the ground laughing like a 12-year-old girl. My God, it was amazing.

But the laughter hurt my love handles, and as I lay on the ground staring at the sky my legs started to seize up.

When I got home I ate two bags of crisps and half a packet of Hobnobs, rendering the entire hour completely pointless. I spent the next three days walking like RoboCop, and didn't return to that game for another 18 months.

Solo Dadding (and a New Level of Respect for My Wife)

As much as I was desperate to be a hands-on dad, so far, Rachel had been there to guide me through everything. I was pulling my weight but she was still project manager. She'd flown solo loads of times since I'd returned to work, but now it was my turn to sample being outnumbered by my babies as she started her contact days back at work. It was a real wrench for her to leave them for a full day. As much as she'd considered herself to be 'ready' to go back to work, especially on those pukey days when she'd undergo more costume changes than Madonna, when the time came to leave the house she got very upset and said that she didn't want to go. I gave her a hug and told her to think of all the cups of tea she'd be able to enjoy while they were still hot and this seemed to cheer her up a little.

I waved goodbye, closed the front door and turned to the lads.

'Right, boys. It's just us. Yeah?'

They seem happy on their mat, I thought. *The kettle's on and there are some biscuits in the cupboard. Get the cricket on, sit back, and enjoy the bonding. I'll prob grab a nap while they sleep actually, feeling a bit tired from last night. You can't beat a daytime kip. Piece of piss, this.*

Maybe I'll watch a few episodes of Homeland *while they're asleep. I can probably polish off the third season if I play it right.*

Ben's kicking his legs a lot today. I'm sure that means something. Is it wind? I hope it's not a poo. He's had three today already. I can't handle any more shit under my fingernails.

So much wriggling. I wish we could harness the energy from it – we'd save a fortune on our gas bill.

The gas bill. We haven't paid it. Shit. Where's that number? It's written on the bill but there's more chance of finding the remote control than any paperwork. The house is a bloody tip. That's not it. That's not it either. What's this? Nursery brochures? Bloody hell, we need to book one soon, or else.

I'll sort that later. They seem too restless. Maybe they're picking it up from me. Time to sing a song. 'The Wheels on the Bus'? Classic. Let's hit it.

I launched into a full-blooded rendition of 'The Wheels on the Bus'.

Well, that kept them occupied for a bit. What next? I don't know any more kids' songs, unless Chas & Dave counts?

They seem ready for a nap now actually. Keep your bloody dummy in, will you? Can't believe how against those things we were till they started screaming. Stroking their heads seems to help. Can I stop yet? No? Yes? No? And . . . they're down.

Right, let's get that telly on! Although I should probably clean the kitchen first. And wash those bottles. And put a wash on. And strip their cots. Better hop to it then. It'll only take five minutes.

40 minutes later.

Jesus, I'm knackered. And that cuppa's gone cold – ugh. I know what I'll do to get some Brownie points: I'll cut Zac's nails. Rachel hates doing that. He's fast asleep so this'll be a doddle. Where are the nail clippers? Bloody nappy bags everywhere.

Yeah, he's definitely asleep. Right, do the little finger first. Nice. Now for the next one. Perfect. This is easy, I should do this professionally. Let's do the thumb. Oh fucking hell, I've cut him. Oh shit shit shit. SHIT. He's crying his little head off. Oh fuck. FUCK. Shit, there's blood everywhere. Definitely a hospital trip, this. Probably a social services visit too. I've failed big-time here. As a human and as a father. I'm a terrible person.

'Don't cry, little man!'

He's in actual pain, this is awful. This isn't hunger or tiredness, this is an open wound. An open wound caused completely by me.

Need to find that cotton wool. BLOODY NAPPY BAGS! Here it is – bit of water and let's stop this bleeding. Okay, it seems to be calming down. Let's just take a peek. And? No, it's still pissing out. Oh Christ, what if he needs a blood transfusion? I'll give him all of mine. Every last drop. Drain me dry like a cured meat. I don't deserve any blood for what I've done.

Okay, he's quietening down now. Although is that a good thing? You need to keep your hand still, little fella! Every time he moves it he starts bleeding again.

I am an awful human.

Collect yourself, Sam. Get a grip.

Yep, I think Ben's waking up now too. Is that crying or gurgling? He's definitely waking up. And it's definitely crying. Probably from all the commotion. Either that or he doesn't want me to have a go at cutting his nails too. Has he pooed? I can't smell anything. Let's try for a sniff. No, nothing. What's that on his arm? Seems blotchy. Maybe it's a phantom poo? It's horrible waking up wet – I did that on a school camping trip once, I wanted to cry then. Best change him pronto.

All the clean clothes are upstairs so gotta make a quick dash. He'll be okay on the sofa for a minute.

I swear these stairs are getting steeper. I've lost count of the number of times I've fallen up them. At least when you fall down stairs you get sympathy – falling up stairs gets you nothing but ridicule. And carpet burn. Haven't slept properly for months. Which clothes are his? This'll do.

Oh my God, did I leave him far enough into the sofa to prevent him wriggling off? I hope so. I'm sure our lads are part lemming.

No, he's fine. Still crying though.

'Breathe, son, breathe!'

I hate it when they do that end-of-days sob, it breaks my heart. And hurts my ears. Don't panic, Sam. Keep calm.

Time to open the nappy. Feel like I'm on Deal or No Deal. *Please make it a good one. That's not a good one. Not at all. Holy Mother of Jesus, that smells like Quavers again. Gonna wretch.*

Where are the fresh nappies? Why aren't they here, where we change the nappies? What is that on his arm? WHERE ARE THE FUCKING NAPPIES? They must be here somewhere. Not nappy bags, Jesus. They don't work anyway, our bin smells like Willy Wonka's U-bend.

Oh, this'll do. Although this brand always leaks, like an old radiator. I'm not running upstairs again. People keep recommending the cloth nappies but I couldn't handle that. I'm all for saving the environment but life's too short for cleaning those things. I've probably indirectly killed a few penguins by adding to the landfill problem, although I'm sure they'd understand if they lived here. Especially with my sons' prolific arses. They produce more crap than Simon Cowell.

Okay. Nappy on. Clothes next. Either this body suit is too small or I'm being a bit shit. Can't fit him in it. Don't want to break his arm for fashion purposes. No, hang on, that's one arm in. Come on, son, help me out here. Wait, is this upside down? How have I managed this? For God's sake, WHY DO THEY KEEP CHANGING THE DESIGN?! Is that a rash on his arm? Balls to this, I'll stick him in a romper suit. Much easier.

Where are the nappy bags? There were millions here a minute ago. Sod it, I'll just wrap it up tight. Like a fajita. The bin stinks anyway.

There we go. Time for a sit-down. I am pooped. Best make a fresh brew as never got round to drinking that last one.

Great, Ben's puked all over his new outfit. I'll say one thing – his timing was impeccable. He should be an assassin. And that is definitely a rash on his arm. Best do the glass-press-check thing. Okay, it's disappearing. That's good. Or is that bad? I've no idea. Better check online. Imagine being a parent pre-Google? It's completely disappeared now anyway. Ah, that's because it wasn't a rash at all – it was a piece of fluff. Brilliant.

Need to clean that sick up. Where's the cloth? The puke cloth? How can that have gone missing, it's the most used item in the house? There it is, let's give that a good scrub. Hmm. Seems to be making it worse. Ah shit, is this the cloth we use for poo? It is! It's the fucking poo cloth – it reeks.

Need to find the other cloth, quickly. Ah, fuck it, I'll just turn this cushion over. No one will know, and it'll dry by the time I have to turn it over again.

And by that I mean when there's another stain.

'It's okay, boys. Don't panic! Daddy's got everything under control. Mummy will be home in another five hours . . .'

5 Things I Learned While the Land of Nod was Closed

1. Phase 2 of parenthood is when an episode of a kids' show comes on and you think, 'Ah fucking hell, I've seen this one.'

2. I now time my morning routine by CBeebies theme tunes. If I'm not running the shower by the time Octonauts is starting, I'm screwed.

3. There's more chance of visiting Narnia than seeing the bottom of your laundry basket.

4. I love my kids more than anything in the world.

5. But I'd love them even more if they'd stop shitting in the bath.

Part 4:

Learning the Ropes

(Because We're Up
Against Them)

I Used to have Standards. Now I Have Kids.

I always wondered what that aroma was – the whiff I smelled when I used to visit friends who had babies.

Now I know.

It's a cocktail of nappies, baby wipes and desperation – and by six months our house reeked of it.

There was shit everywhere. By 'shit' I mean 'stuff', although there was probably a liberal dousing of fecal matter on most objects throughout the house. Crossing our living room made you feel like a contestant on *Total Wipeout*, and, infuriatingly, it was all essential stuff. I had thrown a diva strop the week prior and announced that we couldn't continue under these conditions and we needed to eject any unnecessary items. An hour later I'd put a magazine and a mouldy banana in the bin and rearranged the cushions.

Our kitchen looked like the Monday morning after a music festival – bin bags and disappointment everywhere. If you managed to scramble across all the obstacles between you and the kettle you felt like Edmund Hillary after he scaled Everest. Even then you had more chance of finding a dodo than a mug clean enough to drink from.

Our poor washing machine must have felt like it'd been hit by a truck. Long gone were the halcyon days of bi-weekly gentle washes of tea towels and socks. Nowadays everything was covered with industrial-strength stains, and it was getting spun harder than King Kong's Frisbee three times a day. We bought this thing brand new, promising it happy times in a family home. What we provided were conditions that even the most ardent sweatshop owner would wince at. Maybe it was the sleep deprivation but I'm sure it called me a prick one day during its final spin.

I had nothing to wear because our own clothes didn't get a look-in. Just when they were about to be put into the machine there was always a lorry-load of shit-stained baby sleepsuits ready to jump the queue like a big smelly family who'd bought speedy-boarding tickets. Our clothes were left to sit in the basket, reminiscing about the good old days.

We had a knackered tumble dryer that had worked for two glorious days just after the boys were born before it decided to give up rather than work under this regime. Now we were drying everything indoors on hangers, which had given the house the smell of a wet, stray dog and added to the general obstacle course that blocked all exits and entrances. If burglars broke in I'd only have noticed when they inevitably couldn't find their way back out and had to shout for help.

Then we got the call.

The phone rang, and my wife finally found it beneath the debris. She answered, and what I heard turned my blood cold.

'Pop round? What – now? Yeah, sure! See you in 20 minutes.'

I looked at her with disbelief, hoping this was another wild hallucination caused by lack of sleep. But her eyes said it all – we had visitors on their way.

And these were the worst kind of visitors. The ones you want to impress. Fuckers. Not like your oldest mates who've seen you at your worst and couldn't give two shites. New friends with a clean house, nice clothes, and a quality we seemed to have misplaced amongst the rubble: standards.

What the hell was she doing?

I started to panic. I wanted to shout but the boys were sleeping so I decided to spring into action and find a place on the floor to sob. But I couldn't find anywhere amongst the clutter. And before I knew it my lips were moving.

'We could, maybe, tidy up?'

Eureka!

We both grabbed a bin bag and started shovelling frantically, like we were playing a human game of *Hungry Hungry Hippos*. I took the bins out while she cleared surfaces. I smashed the vacuum round like a maniac while she blitzed the bathroom.

Then we got creative – I slid stuff under the couch and pushed it behind the curtains. I tactically draped the duvet over the dirty clothes in our bedroom. I even turned the sofa cushions upside down to disguise the motley crew of stains we'd collected. We had five minutes before arrival time, and I noticed we still had a kitchen's worth of dirty dishes to get through.

'I'll shove them in the shed! They'll never look there.'

What a beautifully terrible idea.

Our visitors came and all was well in the world. They didn't even visibly wince at the stench as they came through the front door. I tried to encourage them to visit all the key rooms that we'd tidied, but it's not easy to force people into your box room without a good reason.

The important thing was that we hadn't come across like a real-life version of Roald Dahl's Twits.

We went to bed that night filled with happiness and hope for the future.

But 24 hours later we were somehow back to square one. It was as if the tidy up – or creative redistribution process – had never happened.

More stains dramatically appeared on carpets, the volcano of dirty washing continued to spew from our laundry basket, and I couldn't take the bins out as our dustbin was closer to capacity than an early mobile phone that's already received six text messages.

And I couldn't even make a cup of tea because all the cups were still in the shed.

Daddy-Led Weaning

Most parents want their kids to enter higher education or take over the family business. I just wanted mine to stop emptying their arses all over the sofa.

Throughout the first six months, whenever I'd moan about the state of the boys' nappies I'd get warned by other parents to 'wait till they're weaning. That's when business really picks up.'

They'd tell me with the abject terror of a grizzled war veteran talking about his last tour of duty, so I was curious to see just how bad it could get.

Thankfully, after the earlier complications with Zac, both lads guzzled milk like it was going out of fashion. The breast pump was retired after three months' stellar service, and Rachel's bosom breathed a sigh of relief at its leaving party. Rachel stopped me from taking it to the tip as she reckoned we'd get decent money for it secondhand. I thought she wanted to sell it on the dark web to stinking-rich, sexually strange businessmen. She meant at the local nearly-new sale.

We'd got into a decent routine with milk feeds:

Get bottle in
Child drinks
Burp

Puke

Change clothes (baby)

Change clothes (parent)

Continue until end of tether heaves into view

By now it was hard to remember the double feed even being a challenge, like learning to drive.

But parenthood is a crafty bastard. The second you master something it changes the game so you're shit at it again.

It was time to start the weaning process.

There's a process called baby-led weaning, which I'm sure works for some people. 'Baby-led' is the fashionable term in certain quarters – there's even a movement for baby-led potty training, which suggests you dispense with nappies and just get your kid shitting in a bucket straight from the get-go. I'm looking forward to reading about baby-led driving in due course.

We opted to keep our weaning more regimented so we didn't lose our minds. We started off with this specialist baby rice that looked like wallpaper paste. You had to heat it up a little, but I got the timings wrong, quickly learning that shouting 'COOL DOWN, YOU BASTARD' has little or no effect.

You're meant to feed them a bit of bottle milk first before taking it away and offering them a few spoonfuls of this rank-looking stuff. So that's what I did. And they went fucking bananas.

The screaming was so loud that I instantly put their bottles back in their mouths. What a coward. I never had myself down as a parent who'd be bullied by my own kids but that's exactly what happened. A small incident, maybe. But the tip of the iceberg.

If I couldn't even maintain control over a couple of little helpless babies I'd be the kind of dad who gets a 'kick me' sign attached to my back on the school run, probably by my own kids.

Stay strong, I told myself.

I removed the bottles again and it was like I'd opened some ancient Egyptian tomb, all the witchcraft, hexes and incantations stored inside flowing out to wreak havoc on the world.

I put the bottles back in. I was losing this battle quicker than babies lose dummies.

Man up, you wimp.

I took their bottles out and stood firm.

'I AM YOUR FATHER! YOU MAY NOT LIKE WHAT I'M DOING BUT I ONLY HAVE YOUR BEST INTERESTS AT HEART.'

That's what I should have said, if only for my own benefit.

What I actually said was, 'Hang on, lads, hang on. Daddy doesn't know what he's doing here.'

The baby rice didn't look right so I added a bit more milk. I was convinced they'd choke on the rice, so my heart was racing.

I slid a spoonful under Zac's nose and he eyed it warily, like he was doing a Bushtucker Trial. He opened his mouth (probably to get back to good old-fashioned screaming), and I performed what I believe the fencing fraternity call the Forward Lunge, and thrust the spoon inside.

It sat in his mouth for a minute and he looked confused, like he'd just tried a shisha pipe for the first time. He refused to even attempt to chew, which was perfectly understandable considering he didn't know what chewing was.

I went to have a go with Ben but he'd already grabbed his bottle and started drinking from it again, while simultaneously grunting like a mad pisshead who nobody wants to sit next to on the bus.

Much as real history isn't told by monarchs but instead by the everyday folk on the street, so the story of weaning babies isn't told by the feeding, but instead by the nuclear-level shite they start to produce.

The bits of rice and porridge and other proper foodstuffs we'd started feeding them eventually started to work their way down to the other end, which meant our lives would never be the same again. It was around this time that I learned you should always be careful opening text messages from your wife, as it may be a picture of your son's first actual turd. A truly awful sight that made me swell with pride. I can't imagine I'll be able to contain myself if he gets a degree. People give Judy, mother of Andy Murray, loads of stick for being so passionate about her son, but at least he's winning Grand Slams.

The messiest evening in my time so far as a parent came when the boys were just over six months old. The weaning process was bedding in and proper bottom-logs were now more common in our house than hot cups of tea.

'How many poos can you possibly do in one day?' we used to say to the boys. We viewed it as a rhetorical question. They saw it as a challenge.

I arrived home from a gig at half-ten. Rachel helped me get the boys up for their 11 p.m. feed and then she went off to bed.

Both of them had a distinctly shitty smell about them so I changed their nappies and got them started on the milk. About a minute in, Ben started squeezing and straining in that ever-so-worrying way babies do before you realise there's nothing actually wrong with them – they're just having a massive dump.

Prior to weaning I would have just finished the feed, but that was a risky strategy at this point as they'd recently been more leaky than Julian Assange. I noticed some bum mud appearing through his sleepsuit so I decided to quickly change him.

At this stage they couldn't hold their own bottles for very long, so when I stopped to change one of them the feeding pretty much stopped. They were also becoming very curious about the edge of the sofa, like a pair of base jumpers planning their next leap.

When I put Zac down, he wriggled over to the edge and peered down the 12 or so inches to the carpet. He was in total awe, like he was staring deep down into the Grand Canyon, or observing a Renaissance masterpiece. I suppose a £45 IKEA rug is mesmerising to a baby. He tried to wriggle off so I adjusted him and quickly finished changing Ben.

We got back to the milk.

Within 20 seconds, Zac was gurning like one of those old rubber joke faces that you stick your fingers in. I changed him and we got back to the feed for 45 seconds before Ben decided to release the sequel to his poorly received debut single onto the sofa. The feed was paused yet again while I squirted Vanish on cushions and changed yet another nappy. This time we got a good three minutes back into the feed before Zac equalised with an absolute squelcher to make it 2–2.

Just as I was starting to feel my brain about to snap like a pretzel, Ben gave an almighty guffaw and produced the noisiest poo I had heard up to that point. 3–2! And, more importantly, he wasn't just laughing aimlessly. He was laughing *at* something.

The 'something' he found hilarious was the fifth nappy I'd be changing within a 10-minute window, and previously not something I would have been amused by. But the moment he found it funny, it became downright hysterical. We were sharing a joke, a laugh, a moment. I didn't think life could get any better until Zac smashed one into the top corner to make it 3–3.

Now all three of us were laughing. At the same thing. I had never felt so alive.

By the time we all got to bed, Ben had edged it to 5–4. A nine-nappy thriller. The living room stank, there were baby wipes everywhere and a skid mark on the carpet. More importantly, my boys and I had shared an experience, consciously. I'd never been so happy in my entire life.

Cot's the Problem?

When the boys were about seven months old, I spent several nights sitting on a chair between their cots.

Sleep had been in short supply recently. On the back end of a cough and a cold, over the past week the boys had had less shut-eye than an insomniac barn owl who works double shifts at the 24-hour garage. We had experimented with a new Avery house rule – we wouldn't bring them in bed with us unless it was after 5 a.m. and they became unsettled. (Note to reader: if you decide to adopt the 'Avery 5 o'clock Protocol', do be sure to check whether the reason they're crying is because their nappy has leaked BEFORE you absentmindedly let them get between your crisp white sheets. Ugh.) Of course, like most new parents, when the boys were poorly, we didn't apply any of the normal rules. They'd been getting in with us most nights, and they'd quickly got used to the non-stop affection buffet available from my wife and me. They had sampled business class so quite understandably couldn't face going back to economy – but tonight was the night. We had to stand firm. They were going to stay in their own cots.

My wife had mixed fortunes getting them down as I drove back from a gig. They clearly weren't happy and wanted to be moved into our bed again, like a pair of unsettled professional footballers hoping for a big-money move on transfer deadline day. I got home at 2 a.m. and went straight into their room. As soon as I entered, the sobbing stopped and a quiet and respectful calm descended on the room. I felt a bit like the Pope.

I put their dummies in but refused eye contact, thus letting them know the situation, the same way you mumble one-word answers to a taxi driver so he knows you don't want to hear his views on immigration. They accepted the dummies with good grace and for the first time I felt like a strict father from the 1950s. No smiling, warmth or empathy, just business.

I made an abrupt turn and strode out of the room, feeling confident that I'd had a positive effect on proceedings. I felt the warm glow of smugness, so nauseating in others but utterly magnificent when felt by oneself.

I am a brilliant dad, I thought. What a fool.

As I stepped a foot out of their door they both screamed like velociraptors who'd missed their favourite TV show.

Shit.

I went straight back in, determined not to pick them up. I sat on the chair between their cots and started to breathe heavily. Not in a weird way, but I was knackered myself, and thought that maybe I could get some meditation shit going.

They'd gone quiet so I carried on, feeling pretty bloody Zen if I do say so myself. After five minutes I was convinced they'd gone down as the room was completely silent.

I opened my eyes to see both of them staring at me like those twins from *The Shining*.

Bollocks.

I shut my eyes again and counted to 60. When I opened them they were still looking at me as if to say *Your move, bitch*. It was turning into a huge stand-off, our very own Cuban Missile Crisis.

Then the giggling started. I don't care who you are but when your baby starts laughing, you join in. To counter it I launched into a whispered monologue about how it's not always appropriate to laugh, etc., etc., blah, blah. I think I was hoping to bore them to sleep.

In the end they did fall asleep and I got a lovely 40 minutes of shut-eye in a horrible position on the chair that caused my neck to ache for days.

It was getting to that stage where you had to stand your ground.

The Carrot or the Stick

Most of the first seven or eight months of parenting are focused on keeping your child fed, warm and safe. Up to this point you'll probably consider them to be the sweetest human that's ever crawled the face of the earth.

Then you witness them throw a chunky flap book into another kid's face while biting your auntie's ankle, and the penny drops that maybe a bit of discipline wouldn't go amiss. I use the word 'discipline' very loosely. I would never hit my kids, although I can't completely rule out hitting other people's.

I was never smacked as a child and thankfully I have a great relationship with my parents. My mum is the strongest person I know, and my dad has kept remarkably upbeat over the years in the face of some dilapidated (and very painful) body parts letting him down. As long as I wore a coat in the winter because 'it's colder than it looks out there, son' they were totally supportive of everything I wanted to do.

As a teenager I wanted to play music, so they bought me a bass guitar and amp. After seven years of chasing that pipe dream I decided that deep down I'd always wanted to be a comedian, so they let me move back in so I could put my rent money towards driving round the country every night for stage time.

They fostered a belief in me that I could achieve these things. Never a cockiness though – they were always quick to shoot down anything approaching a swagger. My dad has an uncanny knack for bringing me gloriously back down to earth, like any self-respecting northern father should. One time they came to watch me do stand-up as part of a charity gala show where I was alongside other, more successful comedians, many of whom were TV stars.

After the show my mum was singing my praises and, as proud mothers are prone to hyperbole, she was exaggerating by 70-80% how good I actually was.

'You were by far the best, son. I don't understand why you're not on the telly.'

'Thanks, Mum,' I said, nervously smiling to show anyone within hearing distance that I wasn't taking this compliment seriously.

Just in case I was letting it get to my head my dad was quick to point out, 'Maybe it's the shirt, but you looked terribly fat up there, son.'

I was always looking upwards but my feet never left the ground.

So with this solid base, I'd decided what kind of relationship I wanted to have with my children – back when I was childless and naive. They'd see me as their friend, mentor and confidante. Someone they could share a laugh with and come to with their troubles. They'd also hold a healthy fear of me and try to avoid getting on my wrong side. Not that I'd be violent or angry of course, nor even have to raise my voice. Their respect for me would run so deep that just a stern expression or a raised eyebrow would do the trick. Then, after a full apology from them and a declaration that I was correct all along and that they would ensure this would not happen again, we would be back to enjoying each other's terrific company.

What a huge pile of utter horse bollocks.

My boys see me as a climbing frame who occasionally wipes their arses. Nothing more, nothing less. And I'm fine with that.

But as they grew older it became clear that we couldn't let them continue throwing toys at the telly or slapping us in the face without teaching them right from wrong. That meant the odd telling-off was in order. Which I struggled with.

Whenever I raised my voice, they laughed. Sometimes they'd laugh and point at me. Once they both laughed, pointed and said, 'Oh, Daddy!' as if the mere idea of me having any credibility in my own house was so outlandish that it must be some form of adult attempt at humour.

It's hard to keep a straight face when everyone around you is giggling. Even if that giggling is at your own expense.

They say the definition of insanity is repeating the same process and expecting a different outcome. So I tried a variety of different approaches towards discipline. The results were mixed:

- **Talking loudly:** They joined in. I got louder. They got louder. We all started laughing.
- **Talking quietly:** They giggled. I giggled. The moment was lost.
- **Talking quickly:** They fell about laughing. One started dancing. I started dancing. (I knew discipline wouldn't

be my strong point but I never expected it to disinte-
grate into a disco.)

- **Talking slowly:** They went quiet. I thought I was on
  to something. I wasn't – one laughed and the other
  clapped his hands. (Really slowly, almost sarcastically.)

None of this was helped by my wife, normally giggling
behind her hand while I attempted to lay the smack down.
During one Mexican stand-off over an uneaten plate of tuna
pasta, I stated quite firmly to the boys that they 'Either eat
that, or have nothing. There's no choice.'

'But that is a choice,' Rachel piped up.

This was a battle I could not win.

Please, Son, Don't Shit in the Pool

As a new parent, there are several leisure activities you are urged to do with your child. Swimming is high on the agenda. We opted to go to an independent baby pool session at the local baths after nearly losing consciousness when faced with the extortionate price of the 'branded' baby swimming lessons that run across the country.

We were excited! Your first swimming trip is meant to be a landmark family day.

But not like this.

We arrived 40 minutes early because I was anxious about getting the boys changed. Rachel and I took a twin each and went our separate ways.

The communal changing room was pokey and there were no cubicles, but we were first in so I grabbed the best spot in the corner and got to it. My twin for the day, Ben, was in a jovial mood so we got down to it pretty quickly as the other dads and babies started to arrive and pile in. It was soon obvious that this was a very dad-heavy (and, indeed, heavy-dad) activity, as it was taking place at the weekend. I saw someone I knew so we exchanged pleasantries as we removed our clothes in front of each other, ensuring our naked bodies didn't accidentally touch. It was just as awkward as it sounds.

It felt good to walk over to the pool carrying my son. *I'm a good old-fashioned dad*, I thought to myself. *Ready to teach, nurture and be the manly role model that my boys need.*

I dipped my foot into the water and made a noise so high-pitched only dogs could hear it. Fuck me, it was cold. I was expecting it to be like a warm bath but it was icy, like the stare of a rush-hour commuter when you've nabbed the last train seat. I wasn't sure this was good and proper, but all the other parents and kids were already in so, holding Ben tightly, I continued to submerge myself in the water.

Slowly, like a Bond girl in reverse, but bald and with man-tits.

Rachel was already bobbing about in the pool with Zac so we manoeuvred our way next to them. There were about 15 parents, mainly dads, and a middle-aged lady leading the class from the poolside. We all walked round in a circle holding our babies while the instructor told us what to do. The whole scene felt vaguely cultish but we soon got into our stride. The first big test came when we were told to dunk our baby completely under the water. I wasn't sure I liked the use of the word 'dunk' – this woman seemed to be treating our offspring like biscuits. Other than the obvious similarities (if you have one you'll want more and having six is just stupid) I couldn't quite make sense of it.

She also made it very clear that if your baby was hot off the press (or 'newborn' as the experts say) then you really shouldn't be dunking at this stage. This simple instruction was too much for one hapless dad to compute and he instantly submerged his little bundle of joy deep down into the water and held him there, much to the abject horror of his wife at the poolside. The baby was fine but I bet their drive home wasn't – her reaction was frostier than the water.

Me and a few of the other dads exchanged smug glances with a subtext of *Look at that guy. We're not like him. We're in control. We're great.*

Maybe it was this smugness that caused Fate to turn around, lace up her steel-capped boots and kick me square in the bollocks. Either way, in the next 20 seconds I learned an important life lesson: when taking twins swimming you must ALWAYS select the one that's already had a massive dump.

What happened next changed me considerably. As a dad and as a man.

It happened so suddenly. We were having a lovely time. I saw a few bubbles, but there were bubbles everywhere. There's always bubbles in water, right? Then I saw a piece of it. Then another. They were the exact size and shape as a Wispa Duo. My brain told me to quickly grab them and hide them somewhere. My hand told my brain to fuck off – where the hell could I hide a pair of floating turds? If anyone had spotted me ramming a piece of poo into my trunks they'd have quite rightly considered me an international-level lunatic.

For about five seconds we just carried on moving around the pool as if nothing had happened. Then a load more came out. It looked like a squid had released its ink.

The mum behind me very kindly just said 'Ooh' and tried to step out of the way, which is impossible in water. The dirty floaters moved inexorably towards her, in slow motion. Her baby reached out to grab one, which was the point at which I leapt into action, handing my twin to my wife and striding over to the poo zone as fast as I could.

'Sorry, everyone,' I shouted, quickly realising this sounded like a confession. It also drew everyone's attention to the foul scene that was unfolding in the water they were standing in. I reached the anal flotilla and tried to form a safe area around it with my arms. Turning back to face the circle I discovered they weren't a circle anymore, just a disparate group of disgusted people gathered at the farthest corner of the pool, holding their babies with such fear you'd think I was about to throw a plugged-in toaster into the water.

'He normally shits first thing in the morning!' I continued, not grasping the fact that I was now polluting their children's ears as well as the pool with this crowbarred blame-shift onto my son.

I glanced at my son. This made the crowd of traumatised bathers also look over in unison, like they were in the side seats at Wimbledon. My wife was holding him at a safe distance with his back to the crowd. As they looked over he slowly turned his head around like an incontinent horror villain.

And he laughed.

They were utterly appalled, and please forgive my lack of imagination at this juncture but there is simply no analogy in the English language that will do this justice – they literally looked like someone had shat in their pool and was laughing at them.

All four of us got out, dejected and feeling like we'd been sent to the sin bin. The clean-up operation wasn't pretty but we all got dressed and met up back in the car. Not a word was uttered. I put the keys in the ignition and looked at my wife. We stared at each other for a moment.

And then we laughed.

And we continued to laugh until it hurt.

Then we decided we would never go back there again.

Let's Roll

When your baby first arrives, let's be honest, they do nothing other than eat, shit and puke. Of course they look cute, but even that gets boring after a while. Ours were stationary for so long I was tempted to use them as actual stationery. Only as paperweights though; I'm not a monster.

'What the bloody hell are you doing with the boys?'

'Isn't it obvious? Ben's holding down the receipts and Zac's on invoices.'

You put them down and leave the room and when you come back they're right where you left them, like an inanimate object or your nana after a large port.

The first time they roll over, you realise that'll never happen again.

The period between lying still and full mobility is quite a testing one. Obviously, when they're running you ragged that's one thing. But when they want to move and can't quite manage it they get more frustrated than someone who's just overheard a spoiler for their favourite TV show.

Ours were slow to grasp just what the fuck they were supposed to be doing. One didn't really care either. He just lay there while the other one made all the mistakes. During pregnancy, a friend had told me that twins apparently develop really quickly due to healthy competition with each other. The theory was that one would see the other accomplishing something and decide they'd like their own slice of the pie, but with an extra squirt of cream on top. Ideally, this would carry on throughout their lives, and if one became a concert pianist then the other would hopefully end up conducting the orchestra. (Or if one ended up scrubbing urinals, the other would at least mop floors. You get the idea.)

I wondered if spite was a healthy springboard for setting life goals.

Then the health visitor mentioned 'Tummy Time' and I thought she was talking about that moment, normally late on a Sunday evening, when you've been watching the telly for so long that your couch-slouch causes your top to ride up and your disgusting belly to make a cameo appearance. She meant, of course, the important process of putting your baby on their stomach to encourage them to roll over and crawl. This held sway with me: I knew if we left them on their backs we'd be waiting forever for them to try and move. And why not? They had everything they needed – food, attention and some shiny stuff hanging over their faces.

So we bought the special support pillows that look like wacky draft excluders and got some beautifully illustrated Tummy Time books that you place next to your baby to encourage them to have a little roll. They had mirrors, bright colours and fluff. Rachel and I got hugely excited with these books but unfortunately when we placed the boys next to them they managed to look at them with the level of disdain I normally reserve for the latest Piers Morgan tweet.

(Later on the books would get barfed on constantly, which we took as an endorsement. After all, babies can't leave feedback on Amazon, so this was the closest thing to it. Eventually, the pages actually stuck together with the sheer volume of puke that had been emptied onto them. The sad moment of my wife trying to prise open one of the stuck-together-pages and ultimately having to bin the book wasn't helped by a rather crass attempt at humour by myself, likening this to something that may occur in a slightly different context when they're teenagers. Deary me.)

For what seemed like ages, every time we put them on their tummies they'd just lie there, motionless, with their faces flat on the floor, like they'd just done a carpet belly-flop for charity. We'd will them to flip themselves over, then cheer, but they just dribbled and cried into the floor.

As much as I told myself I wouldn't judge my kids by the progress of others, it was difficult not to. Barely a day went by that I didn't receive an email from a different source I'd accidentally signed up to telling me exactly what stage of development my baby should be at. These things were relentless and I didn't find them helpful at all. It's my fault: I signed up for them. But these emails were less welcome in my inbox than news that I'd won another Nigerian lottery.

Emails like this:

4 weeks

Your baby will now be starting to recognise faces and responding to sounds. They should also be writing basic poetry.

6 weeks

By now your baby should be smiling regularly and beginning to understand simple calculus while starting to develop an appreciation of ancient Greek architecture.

8 weeks

Your baby should be holding their head at a 45-degree angle and holding sustained academic discussions on the merits of the feudal system, while producing sketches reminiscent in style of minimalist pioneer Ad Reinhardt. They should also be shitting in the bath regularly.

I know we need benchmarks but can't we let them develop at their own pace?

Life is full of keeping up with the Joneses and being herded into step with everyone else. Let's at least cut our little babies some slack and let them dribble and wriggle their way through their first few months without attaching expectations.

It's one thing to be getting automated emails. To hear these things from other parents is infuriating and unavoidable in this modern world of over-sharing, where every achievement is plastered all over Facebook for all to see. It's hard not to feel a mild panic attack on the horizon when you see another one of your friends' kids on Instagram, doing the conga at seven months old and signing up for the Great North Run before they're one, particularly when yours is still sobbing into the carpet every time you whip the Tummy Time pillow out.

'Are yours not rolling yet? Barnaby was already crawling at six months . . .'

Bully for you, Barnaby. Shame your mother is a complete turd.

Slowly but surely though – with regular Tummy Time sessions, vocal encouragement from Rachel and me, and no small amount of sheer bloody determination from the boys – they both learned how to push themselves from front to back. Although in the scheme of things, that's the easy part.

The hard part for a baby is to roll from back to front. Once they nail back to front then they can basically roll their way around town, getting involved in all sorts of shenanigans. But when only 50 per cent of the rolling is nailed, they just get themselves stuck. So despite achieving something truly remarkable, they still end up face down in a pool of their own snot and tears. Like drinking seven Jägerbombs in one go.

I had the boys on my own one day when they were about eight months old. The twins hadn't yet rolled a complete cycle, and our healthy concern was slowly maturing into a mild dread. Everything seemed to be so delayed.

I went to put the kettle on. I came back into the living room and they weren't on the mat. For one-millionth of a second I panicked, until I noticed they'd both moved about two yards. It was like discovering your dog can play poker.

'FUCKING HELL!'

Stop swearing, I told myself. But this was an amazing milestone and I'd bloody missed it. At least when you pop to the fridge and miss your team scoring a goal they show a replay.

'DO IT AGAIN, BOYS!'

They looked at me like they were a pair of bouncers at closing time and I was trying to get back into the club.

Sorry, mate, show's over. You enjoy your cuppa, though. Hope it was worth it.

A strange realisation washed over me for the next day or so. I could never again know that my kids would be exactly where I left them. That was quite a lot to take in.

Autonomy. Individual choice. Free movement. Suddenly I didn't like these things. Turns out I'm Kim Jong-un.

I was freaking out, like when you trap a spider under a glass and it escapes while you're looking for a card.

Soon after the initial rolls they started rolling everywhere. They'd roll across the room to grab toys, try to roll off the bed and roll onto each other, which normally caused total bedlam. Sometimes they'd roll in unison, like a pair of logs rolling down a hill in a cartoon. They just needed Bugs Bunny running along on top of them.

Other Parents

When you have kids, other parents become your life-line to sanity. Paediatricians talk about the importance of adult–child conversation for development of the child, but what about the importance of adult–adult conversation to prevent total brain disintegration? Too much time with only toddlers for company will see your first adult conversation of the day start with you grabbing the other person's cheeks and blowing a raspberry. To prevent your marbles disappearing like a pube in a hipster's beard you need to at least spend a little time with like-minded folk who aren't bored by your limited conversation topics of sleeping routines, feeding habits and which CBeebies presenter you'd like to get off with.

There's often an unspoken bond between fellow parents, even if you're strangers. When the boys were about seven months old I passed a fellow twin dad in the park who was also struggling to contain his effervescent offspring. We exchanged a few words and wished each other luck. I felt like I was in *Fight Club*.

Sometimes another parent may offer words of encouragement or advice. My advice should you come across this yourself is to listen to them, smile, and then feel free to discount everything they've said. On occasion it may sound condescending or patronising, but it's probably worth remembering that you've only had four hours broken sleep, so your judgement may currently be slightly below par.

I've had numerous interactions when something's been said with good intentions but my interpretation has made me question my abilities as a parent. When the boys were nine months old I was pushing them in their pram up a small hill near our house. If you've ever pushed a pram up a hill, you'll know what a challenge this is – the Royal Marines should include it as part of their basic training. It was windy so my face was scrunched up, but other than that I was having a good day.

Halfway up the hill, a car slowed down next to us with the window down. Thinking it must be someone I knew, I stopped and turned to face them. A random man smiled and shouted, 'Don't worry, pal! It gets easier!' before speeding off.

I'd been having a perfectly good day until that point but obviously to the wider world I looked like I was having some kind of breakdown and was on the verge of putting my kids into care. I'm sure he meant well but I won't lie – a part of me wanted to throw the nappy bag after him.

Obviously there will be occasions when a fellow parent will be fine overall but will then throw in one of the following little gems. Sometimes you'll even hear all these things from the same person. And it's fine to push that person into a hedge.

'Ours have always slept right through.'

Listen, I'm thrilled for you. We all are. It must be wonderful. But see these bags under my eyes the size of grapefruits?

They mean this information is less welcome than a positive STI test. So zip it.

'My little boy loves adventurous food!'
Mine does too! Crayons, Lego and faeces are adventurous, right?

'Let me show you this wonderful picture she drew the other day . . .'
Whilst our own child's artwork is beautiful to us, I'd rather sit on a rail replacement bus than look at someone else's.

'I think your child just bit mine . . .'
The Walking Dead is great but you don't want your kids on it. And how do you react if you haven't witnessed the incident? Deny it and you're instantly that cockwomble parent who can never contemplate that their child would ever do anything remotely wrong. (Obviously the correct answer is 'Yeah, probably. Sorry.')

'Oh, don't worry, it took me a while to lose my pregnancy weight too.'
Hang on, we were talking about the weather! How has this morphed into a critique of my body shape? Plus, I'm a man so this sounds a bit weird.

'Oh, yours hasn't started walking/talking yet? Mine did when they were . . .'
Thanks for this visceral reminder that life is a competition to some people. Although while we're on the subject of

development, when are you thinking of learning some tact? You massive berk.

In my experience, older parents who've done their stint seem to be keen on offering advice, whether it's been requested or not. You can choose to view this in two ways: super helpful or really entertaining.

The helpful ones are true guardian angels, and by that, I don't mean the motorbike gang. I certainly wouldn't want to see my mother decked out in denim and leather. Rachel and I hit the jackpot when mums were being given out as both of them have not only got us through some sticky situations but have even saved us a considerable amount of cash at the local nursery.

The misguided ones should not be taken seriously under any circumstances, but my God, are they fun to listen to.

'Forget that Calpol shite – next time he's coughing, honestly, give him whiskey. Not loads, mind. Just a few swigs. Did it with all seven of mine and most of them turned out fine. The ones I still talk to anyway.'

Date Night and the Parenthood Effect

Young kids make you feel like you're under house arrest. But instead of armed guards or electronic tags to keep you in place, you've got a feeding regime stricter than the Khmer Rouge and the energy levels of a diabetic sloth that's cutting out caffeine for Lent.

Rachel and I hadn't been out together for AGES – the last time we'd had a proper date night Donald Trump was just a reality-TV star and Rolf Harris was a national treasure. It had been a while.

'Fancy going out?' she asks.

'The soft play centre will be closed now won't it?'

'No, silly. Me and you. On the tiles. Like the old days.'

'But what about the kids?'

'Your mum can babysit. Come on, it's been ages!'

I agree that we need a night out so I phone my mum and we make some plans. Instead of cruising bars and hitting a club, we buy tickets for a show and book a table at our favourite restaurant.

We get dressed in the only stain-free clothes we have. The excitement in the taxi is unbearable. I feel like I'm off on a mad night out in my early 20s. Anything could happen tonight. Absolutely anything. (As long as we're home for

10.30 p.m., don't get too drunk, and the boys settle okay for Grandma – absolutely anything could happen.)

The restaurant is the same one we went to on our first date, all those years ago. Back then we gazed into each other's eyes and talked about our plans for the future. This time we complain that the wine is making us tired and I pick a speck of what is quite probably shit from my fingernails with a cocktail stick.

I quickly check my phone to see if the boys are down yet but there's no message from Mum. We polish off the booze in record time, more through hysteria than any actual enjoyment. (I drank more when I was 15 than I have since the boys were born, so my alcohol tolerance has dropped lower than a skateboarder's jeans.) I'm slurring my words slightly, but I feel disproportionately proud of disguising this by choosing syllables that require less effort.

I check my phone again. Still nothing from Mum so I text her.

ARE BOYS DOWN YET? Xx

As we pay the bill and trudge across to the theatre I secretly wish we could just fuck off home to bed.

Not for anything dirty, mind. Just a lovely sleep. (Although as a new parent, I view sleep in the same way that pubescent Sam viewed sex – I'm often thinking about it, I don't get as much as I'd like, and I'd happily do it on a bus.)

We head straight to the theatre bar before the show, neck another glass of wine each, and rather optimistically order more for the interval.

We take our seats. The show starts. My wife's head is on my shoulder. *That's nice,* I think. Quality time together. Ten minutes later she hasn't moved and is now starting to slump. *She's only bloody fallen asleep!* I think incredulously, as I rest the side of my head on top of hers.

Next thing I know, the house lights are on and everyone around us has either gone or is getting up. Instinctively I start applauding, quickly realising that I'm at least a minute late to show any appreciation for the performance I just snored through. My misplaced clap solo wakes my wife up suddenly and she looks confused and slightly panicked, like someone who's just sent a text to the wrong person.

We get to our feet on the second attempt and make our way towards the exit. We're not sure if the show has finished or if it's just the interval. I mutter something about not understanding the plot but say it far too loud and become aware that people are now staring at me. There's a piece of toilet paper stuck to the bottom of my shoe.

We deduce that it must be the interval as people are heading to the bar. We have a decision to make.

When we were a new couple we went to Stratford-upon-Avon to go and see *King Lear* at the Royal Shakespeare Theatre. Without wishing to come across as a philistine, it was the biggest pile of shite I have ever seen. The interval came after an epic hour and 45 minutes. Long afterwards we both admitted we had wanted to leave during the interval but didn't want to appear uncouth in front of our brand-new flame. There is no such ceremony here, just a bullet-quick 'Let's get off?'

'Deffo.'

I check my phone. Texts from my mum start flying in as we get outside and the signal returns.

THEY'RE BOTH SCREAMING.

Followed by another:

STILL SCREAMING.

And finally:

FAST ASLEEP NOW.

We follow their example (minus the screaming) and have another little snooze in the back of the taxi, arriving home feeling refreshed and invigorated by our mad night out.

It is 9.35 p.m.

Crying at the
Nursery Gates

At 11½ months it was time to take the twins to nursery for the first time. There were a few tears, but after a while I managed to compose myself and get up off the floor.

Arf.

I jest, of course. It was more complicated than that.

The nursery staff came over and gave the boys a friendly smile and, very impressively, knew which twin was which. My wife handed Ben over as the knot in the pit of my stomach (which wasn't there 10 seconds before) tightened.

Zac started crying immediately. Normally when he cries it's because he's tired or hungry or he's done a poo the size of his head. But this was a different cry. This wasn't whiney – this was desperate. There was real, adult emotion in his sobbing. He sounded like he'd been betrayed. As tears streamed down his face he shot me a look that seemed to say *I trusted you. We had something. But you've brought me here. A strange place where I don't know anyone. How could you?*

I was aware that graphic interpretation of his crying wasn't doing anyone any favours so I quickly turned to Ben in the hope that he'd have already settled in, having been there now for a full 25 seconds.

Someone had sat Ben down on the floor, facing away from me. He still had his coat on (clearly outing him as a newbie) and all the other kids had scrambled round to get a closer look at the fresh meat.

Some were crawling, a few were standing up, one was even doing a rather unsettling arse-shuffle that I'd previously only seen dogs do. But they had one thing in common – they were all staring at him.

Staring in the way that only kids can. Wide-eyed and with enough intensity to cook an egg.

There was no malice there, clearly, but my God it was intimidating. *Don't show any weakness, son,* I thought to myself, before remembering that this was an Ofsted-approved nursery, not a high-security prison.

The staring continued but Ben stared back. Some of the regular crew grew bored and went back to their daily tasks of nose-picking and raspberry-blowing. A small victory perhaps, but I felt a huge jolt of parental pride as I watched my son settle into his new surroundings with all the ease of a foot into a comfy old slipper. Unfortunately I hadn't been that wrong about something since I accidentally brushed my teeth with Anusol at Glastonbury in 2004.

He slowly turned his head towards me and I knew I'd been premature when I could see his bottom lip protruding from his face like a misplaced bratwurst sausage. He did one of those extended inhales that babies do when they're preparing for an extra noisy bawl – it seemed to last longer than the Leveson inquiry – and he let rip with a scream you could cut diamonds with.

At this point I made the executive decision for us to leave the room. The whole scene was beginning to resemble something from *Kramer vs. Kramer* and another kiss goodbye would've been like throwing petrol on an emotional chip-pan fire. I grabbed my wife like a presidential bodyguard in the midst of an assassination attempt, and we fought our way through the empty corridors until we were outside in the rain. I think it was raining – it might have just been Ben's tears.

We got into the car feeling strangely grown up. Our babies had become, if not quite little boys yet, significantly older babies. Rachel opened the small gift bag the staff had given her – it contained a packet of tissues and a couple of biscuits. What a beautiful gesture. And perfectly judged as Rachel was beginning to weep. I secretly wanted tissues too but made do with a chocolate digestive. We looked at each other and tried to convince ourselves they'd be alright. After all, it was only a day at nursery, right? Then we realised we had another conundrum to contend with. What on earth would we do with ourselves for the next seven hours?

We could do pretty much ANYTHING for the WHOLE day. No nappies, no bottles. Just us.

Scary. What the fuck would we talk about?

It's My Party and
I'll Cry If I Want to

Despite it feeling like a mere fortnight had passed since they were born, my beautiful boys were about to turn one. Where did that year go?

The most frequent comment from other parents since they'd arrived was a variation of the old cliché 'They grow up so fast, you know.' It grew mildly annoying. Now I had started saying it.

The milestones of that first year had been both exciting and terrifying. Their first smiles, laughs and eye-gouges all brought me to tears for a variety of reasons. Putting their toothbrushes next to ours for the first time felt weird, as if real people had moved in rather than the little babies that were squatting in the nursery. Every time they moved up a nappy size I could feel time slipping through my fingers like sand. I had moved their cots down to the lowest rung setting earlier in the week and my heart ached even more than my back. The way it was going they'd be married by summer and choosing my care home by Christmas.

But what a year! There'd been more ups, downs, shit and screaming than a novelty rollercoaster through a farm. And even though I'd managed to physically age seven and a half years in just 12 months, we'd survived. There was much to celebrate for Rachel and me, but not least the fact that it was our boys' first birthday.

The last birthday party I'd organised was my own 30th. I didn't really organise it either – I invited a load of people to a bar over Facebook and we got pissed. Easy peasy. This was a slightly different animal.

When your children first arrive, they don't understand when it's their birthday and therefore treat it just the same as any other day. So in reality, we could get away with doing nothing. Rachel also made a very good point that visitors and presents could be a distraction from our (not-always) well-oiled routine. Yet in spire of this – and the fact I've always been completely reviled by TV shows like *My Super Sweet 16* – now it was our kids' birthdays, we wanted to spoil them rotten.

But who do you invite to a thing like this? The boys certainly didn't have any friends yet, unless you counted each other and possibly Rachel and me – although even that was stretching it on the days they'd look at me like they were my landlord and I was their tenant in arrears.

So do you just invite all your usual mates? I didn't really want Baz and all the boys from footy rocking up with a load of cans, turning the air blue with stories of booze and chasing women.

'You should've seen it, Sam. I got so wankered that I totally forgot I'd taken her mate home the night before. So when we go down for breakfast, there's a bit of an atmosphere at first, but as it turns out they're both a bit *curious*, if you know what I mean. So I'm going round to see 'em both again tomorrow night!'

'Wow. That's quite something. [Bullshit, but something nonetheless.] Did I tell you that my son smiled at me last week and it made me feel completely at one with the universe?'

I'm not sure they would have fitted in.

So we sent the invites out to friends and family (omitting Baz and the footy boys) and started getting ready to celebrate.

It's the day of the party. We get up early (as if that needs mentioning) and get the lads eating their breakfast. We're keen to try to make the day as normal as possible for them to avoid any wobblers being thrown.

The house, as you've come to understand is common for the Averys, is a complete bombsite although in fairness, that's possibly a bit unfair to most bombsites. Whatever the rights and wrongs of bombs, at least they're *supposed* to fuck things up. Our house is *supposed* to be a half-decent-looking semi-detached, not a shit-smelling halfway hostel for lunatics.

The house doesn't just need a tidy-up. It needs a proper clean. This isn't something you can bluff your way through in 20 manic minutes while humming the Benny Hill music. We need the whole morning to steam, polish and scrape our way to respectability.

It's my job to clean and tidy; Rachel is on food and beverages. She also wants to bake two cakes in the shape of buses. I gently suggest that we should purchase the cakes in order to take the pressure off her. She is having none of it. I then even more gently float the idea that maybe one cake would be enough, seeing as the boys wouldn't know either way. She playfully throws a bottle of bleach at my head and tells me to 'stick to your fucking job and I'll fucking stick to mine'. You can't beat a good bit of banter.

So while the boys are napping I start on the kitchen floor with the steam cleaner. It's all guns blazing for 30 steamy seconds, and then it decides that enough is enough and it's time to pack up. I can't blame it – I've been working this poor thing to the bone like a Victorian pit pony, and clearly given the choice between cleaning our rancid floor one more time and death, it opts to join the great big Cash Converters in the sky.

So I jump on the floor with a pack of floor wipes and start scrubbing away, scratching at any stubborn bits of porridge that have become encrusted like stalagmites on the lino. After 10 minutes the floor looks so good you could definitely eat your dinner off it (or, indeed, throw your dinner on it).

Next is the bathroom, and despite taking care to close the door quietly and tiptoe around, I manage to drop a rubber duck onto the hard floor, which bounces like a rugby ball out of my grasp. Unfortunately, this isn't just any old rubber duck, it's a battery-operated TALKING rubber duck. Unluckily for me, its batteries are on the way out, which renders its quack a couple of octaves lower than factory standard. So the duck bounces across the floor, sounding like a demented goose making threats towards me, until it hits the door and wakes one of the boys up. Whenever one of them woke up unexpectedly, Rachel and I would become a mini SWAT team. It was imperative to get to the target (crying child) immediately, to either neutralise (put dummy back in) or extract (er, extract) them from the situation.

I dive silently into their room to rescue Ben's dummy, but forget that I'm still wearing rubber gloves that are laced with bleach and other cleaning products. As I reach out for the dummy I spot my yellow hand and decide I should probably take them off, so tiptoe quickly back into the bathroom, accidentally knocking the duck across the floor again. This kickstarts another baritone rant from the low-powered novelty aqua bastard. This does not sit well with Ben, who seems to purposefully scream louder, and maybe even tilt his head towards Zac's ears, causing him to also wake up.

Now they're both yelling and thrashing around in their cots so I remove the Marigolds, like a Chippendale whipping those special Velcro kecks off, and dive back into the boys' room. It was vital they got a half-decent nap, otherwise they'd be the worst party hosts since Hannibal Lecter appeared on *Come Dine with Me* but they've both got a look in their eyes that says, *Father, there's more chance of us boarding the next NASA flight to Mars than going back to sleep*, so I get them up and take them downstairs.

There's something about having guests on their way round that makes you notice all the really grubby areas of your house that you didn't even know existed, let alone needed a good scrub.

Rachel is progressing well with her ambitious double-decker bus cake in the kitchen as I ferry the boys back downstairs after their failed nap attempt. Sticking the telly on to keep them occupied I try to work my way round the grubby nooks and crannies before anyone arrives. I'm aware that our guests will be arriving soon, and when I get stressed I tend to eat. (If I worked on the stock market I'd be the size of a blimp.) I notice that Rachel has put some leftover cake near the sink, so like a total scruff I pick it up and, without batting an eyelid, take a massive bite out of it.

'WHAT ARE YOU DOING?!'

'Erm . . .' Crumbs are falling from my mouth.

'THAT'S ONE OF THE BUSES!'

'Oh shit. Is it? I'm so sorry.' I'm now chewing furiously so that I can try to speak properly.

'YOU'VE BITTEN HALF THE BONNET OFF!'

'Oh God. What have I done? It'll be okay. Couldn't we say it's been in a pileup?'

'IT'S A FIRST BIRTHDAY PARTY! WE CAN'T HAVE A CAKE THAT'S BEEN IN AN ACCIDENT!'

I fear that I'm also about to be in an accident involving my private parts and the electric whisk, but thankfully the doorbell rings and I'm saved. Rachel's mum comes in and gets to work fixing the cake with some creative positioning and a shedload of icing. (And it turns out it doesn't matter because the guests are too polite to say anything about it. To our faces, anyway).

Close friends and family come along to share our celebration. The boys don't quite know what to make of it and get a little bit tired and grumpy. When we sing 'Happy Birthday' to our little boys who are now a whole year old, all four of us have tears in our eyes (although the boys handle their tears in a slightly more audible manner to Rachel and me).

THE SECRET DIARY OF A ONE-YEAR-OLD

Turned one today. Didn't think I'd feel any different. But I do. More angry, more entitled. And even more confused. But mainly angry. Not sure what at either, which makes me even more angry. And confused. Basically, don't mess with me, okay? Had a birthday party, which I thought were supposed to be enjoyable. Loads of people I don't know turned up at the house and brought kids with them who played with my toys all day. How is that fun? Then every single person stared at me while singing this proper creepy song, as Mummy lunged towards me with fire. Fucking terrified, I was. Think next year I'll just have a quiet one.

Time Flies (and Babies Crawl, Eventually)

The boys were 13 months old when it finally happened. We'd witnessed so many almosts and nearlys that we knew it was going to happen soon, but when it finally did it was completely out of the blue. We were all in the lounge, except for Ben who'd rolled himself into the hall. I could hear him grunting and gurgling so I knew he was safe and assumed he was probably filling his nappy, maybe opting for a bit of privacy instead of eyeballing us like he normally did. We were staring at the television, then I noticed movement in the corner of my eye – and there was Ben, crawling into the room at some pace, a smile on his face the size of East Anglia. Rachel and I erupted like we'd seen the most amazing magic trick, and he started to giggle as he raced across the carpet.

'Where's my phone?' I shouted, desperate to capture this moment for posterity.

He motored through the lounge, then his smile transformed into a frown as he crashed straight into the wall. It was like he'd hotwired a car but didn't know how to steer or apply the brakes. He slumped to the floor and started crying.

We picked him up and he did another length of the lounge before calling it a day, totally shattered.

Soon after, Zac joined the party and every morning I was followed round the house like a mother duck, my two boys chasing after me on all fours.

The difference it made to our lives was astounding. Previously the boys had got really angry and frustrated at not having any independence. Now they were charging round the house, finding all the danger zones in a house that definitely wasn't toddler-proofed yet. And they were relentless. If I worked in risk assessment I'd save my company loads of money by getting rid of the Health and Safety team and just employing a couple of crawling babies to sniff out all the hazards.

I have never witnessed anything on this planet as fearless as a baby who's just learned to crawl. That look on their face as they crawl towards you – a weird mix of confusion, pride, concentration and joy – will stay with me forever.

But despite the exposed plug sockets and unlocked cupboards, the biggest danger you face with two mobile pipsqueaks is the new 'interactive' nappy changes you have to contend with. I had just got to a competent standard of changing if I was left completely unfettered. Now I had to deal with fending off sneak attacks at the crucial moment from a newly nomadic baby who just wanted to get involved.

We had a changing table but it was upstairs, and now they were roaming around the house like a pair of PacMen it wasn't safe to leave either of them unattended.

On one occasion I decided to do a change in the lounge, grabbing the changing mat and laying Ben down. He instantly wanted to get up and crawl off to explore the area behind the TV cabinet. I told him that he'd done a poo and needed changing. He pointed at Zac with real authority, incredulously trying to blame his brother for the mess that was now trickling down his leg.

I laughed. The boys laughed. But then everything's a laugh until someone gets shit in their mouth, isn't it?

Using enough force to keep Ben in place but not so much that it caused him any distress, I managed to remove his rancid nappy. The stench hit me right in the eyes and I recoiled, momentarily throwing my head back in disgust. Big mistake. By the time I looked back down, Ben had crawled away from my reach, waggling his shit-splattered rump at me as he shot towards the doorway.

'NO!' I squawked, feeling desperate. Unfortunately, like most babies when they crawl off with enough bum mud on their arsecheeks to launch their own compost collective, he wasn't in the mood for authority, and he giggled and guffawed as he left the room and disappeared out of view.

I jumped up to grab him and it was only when I reached the doorway that I realised I'd left the open dirty nappy on the mat in the room with Zac. I spun around and saw Zac slowly crawling towards it, like a hungry dog approaching his dinner.

This must be stopped.

I looked back at Ben and he was now in the hallway, about to plonk his obscene buttocks onto the carpet.

This must also be stopped.

If this was one of Aesop's Fables, there'd be a beautiful conclusion to this story and an inspiring message about human behaviour. Unfortunately, it's neither of those things and the ending isn't pretty.

I could have stopped either one of them committing a fecal crime. But I didn't. Forced to choose, I froze. I stood in the doorway, unsure of which incident to prevent. Because of this, both incidents happened.

Ben sat down on the floor and started to bounce, pretty much wrecking a full square foot of carpet in the process. And Zac poked his finger into the bum sludge and momentarily looked at it, before placing it onto his tongue.

'NO! PLEASE, SON! DON'T!'

Thankfully, the taste repulsed him. Unfortunately, as he tried to get rid of the foul taste he used the same finger and accidentally smeared even more onto his tastebuds.

I learned that, just like the Third Reich, I couldn't fight a war on two fronts.

While I surveyed the catastrophes in front and behind me, Ben had crawled over to his favourite noisy toy and was repeatedly pressing the button that made it say 'WELL DONE!', which couldn't have been more inappropriate.

I cleaned Zac up first, before dealing with Ben and then the carpet.

With some distance, this story amuses me. At the time I felt utterly useless.

The other thing Rachel and I were desperate for a sniff of was words. Everyone talked about this mythical 'twin language' but we'd not seen any real communication between the two of them yet. There'd been the odd moment when they'd looked at each other and it seemed as if they were going to suddenly start a full-scale conversation or break into song.

I was convinced they were having full-blown conversations every time I left the room. Sometimes I'd walk in and they'd give me that look you do when the person you've been slagging off turns up.

'He's just a bit dull, isn't he? Remember last week when he made us laugh for five minutes by putting the blanket over his head? Yeah, well he fucking burned that out quickly, didn't he? Kept doing it all week to the point where I just started bawling. Same thing happened with Peekaboo. How can you possibly ruin that game? Oh shit, here he comes. Back to the baby talk.'

'You okay, boys?'

'Goo-goo, ga-ga . . .'

I was also convinced they were egging each other on to use the wrong words. Every time we'd try to correct them, it felt like they were pulling each other to one side. 'Don't listen to him, he hasn't got a clue. Have you seen what he's wearing? He's an idiot, mate. So next time he pronounces it *bus* just remember, it's *rowrow*. Okay?'

One such example was when the boys were nearly two, when Ben suddenly started counting to three all on his own, until Zac kept shouting 'NINE!' at him and he bowed to peer pressure and also decided that in fact, nine was the only number he required.

But for the main, their communication was all in my imagination. Quite often, before they could crawl, I'd put one of the boys down on the playmat, and the one already on the floor would get quite excited at the prospect of another baby joining them. When they realised it was the same baby as always they managed to look really disappointed, as if they'd ordered fish and chips and a green salad had been brought to their table.

We tried all sorts to get them to communicate – lying them next to each other, on top of each other, waving them about, holding them next to each other while we made them dance, as if simulating the awkward feel of a school disco would help.

Ben was crawling all over the place but Zac was still happy to just chill. He was sitting up quite well at this stage, looking a bit like an infant Buddha, but without the joss sticks and Zen attitude.

It was the morning and we were frantically trying to get everything ready for nursery. Zac was really upset about something and it's difficult to know what once you've checked the key areas.

Have they leaked? No.

Have they puked? No.

Are they hungry? Doubt it.

Are they thirsty? No.

Sometimes I wondered if the whole concept of being alive was just getting a bit much for them. Being born must be like getting out of your tent at Glastonbury – one minute you're nestled cosily and the next you're thrust into a world of strange sights, sounds and smells where nothing makes sense and everyone's talking bollocks.

I often feel like crying when I can't install the software update on my smart TV, so I can't imagine I adjusted well to being alive when I was born.

So I'd gone through my mental checklist of what the problem could be, plus I'd verbally asked him if any of these things were bothering him.

'What's going on, mate?'

We always speak to our babies, because it's the right thing to do, but it's always a one-way conversation. Probably a good thing because his reply would doubtless be along the lines of *Father, I'm a toddler. I haven't got a fucking clue what's going on. My little head is jammed up my arse, metaphorically speaking.*

So Zac continued to cry, with each shriek louder than the last. It was horrible to see him like this. Apparently Ben thought so too – he spied a stray dummy on the other side of the room and, like a hawk spotting a rogue field mouse, shot over to retrieve it. He crawled back to us and, slightly out of breath from his little sojourn over to the skirting board, lifted the dummy up for Zac.

He popped it into his mouth and Zac instantly settled.

No words were needed.

At that point the room seemed to get slightly dusty as I felt my eyes getting moist. I looked up to see Rachel standing in the doorway, tears in her eyes, having witnessed the whole beautiful exchange.

We embraced, tears of joy rolling down our cheeks like at the end of *Rocky*.

This crawling thing was brilliant.

Controlled Crying

Being a parent requires you to make difficult decisions. Like being an elite football coach, most of these decisions are made under stressful conditions when it often feels like everyone else thinks they know better.

Every parent has to make decisions for their children – and every child responds differently, so it's dangerous to assume there is a 'one size fits all' solution for anything. This is parenting, not condoms.

For many, the idea of leaving your child to scream themselves into Slumberland is totally barbaric. For others, it's an option worth exploring, albeit tentatively.

We'd spent the first 12 months as a pair of sleep-butlers to our boys. Whenever they woke up we'd be right by their side with a menu of options.

'How can I help you today, sir? I have a delightful selection of fresh dummies that might interest you, or maybe a bit of hand-holding until you drop off, if that would be more agreeable? A cuddle? Certainly, sir. Excuse me, sir. I'm terribly sorry to bother you but it appears you have pissed everywhere, sir. If you would allow me the opportunity to change your sopping nappy and clothes then I do believe you'll have a much higher chance of reaching the Land of Nod.'

This devotion to helping them drop off caused two things:

1. The boys would never get back to sleep without one of us sat with them.
2. Our evenings were more disrupted than a china shop on the route of the Pamplona bull run.

Out of context, number 2 might sound rather selfish. But if you've got kids you'll know that without any proper relaxation time, it's no exaggeration to say that you become a *much* shitter parent. Tempers are frayed, good judgement disintegrates, and, henceforth, giving your kids the full attention they require during the day is impossible. Your brain becomes a car engine slowly being eroded by the battery acid of exhaustion.

Rachel was reading an article shared on one of the Facebook baby groups she'd joined.

'Have you heard of controlled crying?'

I was skeptical at first. I thought it was some New-Age self-help session she'd seen on Groupon. One where we all stand in a circle holding hands with hippies and sobbing together for 20 minutes. The last voucher-site activity she'd dragged us to was hot yoga, and I hadn't enjoyed that after the elderly lady on the next mat had dripped all over me during a particularly sweaty pose.

Without even knowing the specifics, I dismissed it.

'Not for me. I prefer to keep my crying completely uncontrolled,' I said, and went back to scrolling through my phone.

'It's not for you,' she explained. 'It's for babies.'

She explained how it worked – you resist the urge to pick up and comfort your child when they cry after bedtime and this helps them learn to self-soothe. I was appalled.

There was no way I was leaving my little boys to scream and sob, forcing them to feel alone and forgotten about. It made me feel deeply sad just thinking about it. Of course, if they were still crying in their mid-to-late 20s I'd probably give it a go then, but right now they were still my little babies.

'Apparently it really helps them sleep.'

This changed everything. They hadn't been sleeping well, and as a result we were more tired than the wallpaper of a Blackpool guesthouse.

Anything was worth a try, I reasoned. Especially as my last attempt at changing their bedtime routine (saying 'Please go to sleep' in a variety of desperate voices) had met with mixed results.

Anyway, they wouldn't be alone technically, as I'd be stood right behind the bedroom door. Sure, *they* wouldn't know I was there, but *I'd* know I was there.

I agreed to give it a trial.

We bathed and dressed them as they played with their willies. We gave them their milk and then put them to bed. I read them a story and kissed them both goodnight. Everything was normal. Then I stood up and left the room. I couldn't help but turn my head to look at them as I walked out and they both looked absolutely horrified: *And just where in the name of fuck do you think you're going, Jeeves?*

They didn't make a noise though, and when I got onto the landing they were still silent.

'Nailed it,' I whispered to myself, just as both of them exploded into a fit of violent screaming that must have registered on the Richter scale.

One thing that Rachel and I had agreed on was that if we were going to try this, we had to stand firm. There's no point doing it half-arsed since then there'd be no chance of a silver lining to the miserable cloud that was forming above our house.

So I stood outside their bedroom door against my better instincts, feeling hollow and despondent as they fluctuated between yelps of despair and cries of agony.

I didn't just feel like a bad parent, I felt positively evil. Regardless of the motives, I'd just deserted my kids and walked away when they needed me. In terms of terrible parenting, this was up there with missing sports day or forcing them to support Everton (which I'll be doing by the way).

I could undo all of this by taking three steps back into their room but I knew I had to be strict – with myself more than them.

Don't cave, Sam. Don't be a coward.

Two minutes went by and it was time to go back in.

Thankfully, most toddlers are as loyal as a pet dog and my entrance was greeted by an abrupt end to the crying and smiles all round.

They both looked at each other as they lay back down and seemed to be saying, *He must have just forgotten something and gone to retrieve it. Thankfully, that ugly episode is firmly behind us and we can now return to the normal routine.*

I stood up to leave the room again but before I'd fully straightened my legs, they knew I was going. They erupted like I had never seen before, flinging themselves around their cots like a pair of aggressive trout, whacking into the sides and banging their heads on their mattresses like lunatics.

I dragged myself out of the room but this time I had to wait four minutes before I could go back in. I sat at the top of the stairs with my head in my hands wanting to cry myself. Was this heartache worth it?

And what the fuck was so 'controlled' about any of this? As I left the third time the entire scene was more hysterical than a Sicilian funeral.

At one stage they both suddenly went so quiet that it shat me right up. I crept in to check they were okay and they both jumped up screaming like it was a really angry surprise party.

This continued until we got to the eight-minute mark, by which point I was about to cave in and go and sit with them, despite being very aware that if you were going to do this you either had to fully commit or not bother in the first place.

Did other parents have these moments of doubt? I now fully understand that they do. But as I sat at the top of the stairs I felt completely clueless. What should I do? What was the answer?

They'd gone quiet a few times already before starting up again, like the annoying house alarm of a neighbour who's gone away for a fortnight.

But this time they were totally silent, and I was sure I could hear snoring on the baby monitor.

I tiptoed in, carefully dodging all the squeaky-floorboard hotspots, to see them both sleeping like, well, babies. (By the way, floorboards are noisier after 8 p.m. – fact.)

I adjusted their duvets and told myself that I knew they were okay – they were in a warm and safe cot after a lovely day filled with love and cuddles. I kissed them goodnight and felt a small pang of achievement. That had been a really tough experience but I'd struggled through it.

This approach isn't for everyone. Some parents refuse to do it and I hardly blame them, but it definitely worked for us. Over the next six months we'd use it when required and hardly ever went past the four-minute mark.

My Toddler Won't Eat and It's Stressing Me Out

[Finishes making lunch.]

Okay, food is ready. God, that took me ages. Is it even worth it? I suppose we'll find out.

He NEEDS to eat this meal. How can anyone survive on toast? Toast and biscuits. He's like a bloody student already.

Wish he'd stop screaming. Although he's probably hungry – he hasn't eaten properly all week.

I'm not gonna give him a drink yet, sometimes that puts him off. I think it does anyway. Maybe it just puts me off? What if he's thirsty though? I know, I'll make the drink but hide it on the other side of the oven. Perfect.

Now, shall I have the food ready for him on the table when I put him in his seat? Or should I bring it over when he's sat down, like a dishevelled waiter?

Too many choices. Feel like I'm cracking a puzzle.

[Puts son in highchair.]

He's crying already. Haven't even shown him the food yet. Must be because he's hungry, right?

I'm nervous. This is more stressful than a credit check.

Here we go – smiley face, happy singing and now for the big reveal . . . TUNA LASAGNE!!!

[Son screams even harder.]

Oh, fuck. That's a bad start. He does like this stuff though. Maybe he's forgotten. Let's get a little spoonful first shall we? Here we go and . . .

[Son turns his head away from the spoon.]

Oh fuck. Fuck. Fuck. Fuck. Not again. Stay calm, he'll sense it. Show him the bowl.

[Son glares at food.]

Christ, he looked at that food like it owed him money. Not a great sign. Might as well try the aeroplane spoon trick.

[Does aeroplane spoon trick.]

Nope. Never works. Don't even know why I still try it. Even when I was a baby I remember thinking that was shit.

If I can just get him to taste it, he'll remember he likes it.

Fair play to him, he's a stubborn little sod. That'll help him go far in life. I think. Will it? Or is it the worst quality you can have? Either way, he'll need to eat the odd meal whatever he does.

THAT DOESN'T MATTER RIGHT NOW! Let's just get him to eat this small and lovingly prepared portion of fucking lasagne.

Is it too hot? Too cold? Too just-the-right-temperature? I didn't realise Goldilocks was based on true events.

Let's try the dummy move. I'll hold the dummy out, he'll open his mouth and then BOOM – I'll switch the dummy for a spoon of tasty, nutritious food. Never fails.

Here goes.

[Tries dummy trick.]

Well, that was a fucking disaster. I'm wearing more food than he's eaten in the last two days.

Need to calm him down.

'It's okay, little man! Don't worry, Daddy's just getting a bit worried about you. Would you like some food?'

[Son screams until he starts coughing.]

I think that's a no.

He's not accepting a small spoonful, might as well go for a massive one.

[Heaps spoon up.]

What a surprise, that didn't work either.

I just need to get some food into his mouth. He'll taste it and everything will be fine.

[Moves spoon towards son's mouth, son bobs and weaves like a prize fighter avoiding a jab.]

This isn't what I expected. All those books I read, where was the chapter entitled 'Force-Feeding Your Screaming Child While You Hold Back Your Own Tears'?

Sometimes I think it'd be easier to plug him back into his mum for a few days.

Let's have another go. My God, this is impossible. Should be a parlour game: 'Hey, guys! Who fancies a quick round of Feed the Uncooperative Baby with me?'

It'd make a great iPhone game.

What if I hold the spoon still – will he accidentally move his mouth onto it?

[Son screams blue murder until a small particle of lasagne touches his lip and then he stops, considers the situation momentarily and then opens his mouth.]

YES! We're in. Come on! Feel like I've cracked a safe.

[Loads big spoonfuls in as quickly as possible, making up for lost time.]

Must maintain eye contact. Don't change sitting position. Keep everything EXACTLY as it is till he's finished. Any change in circumstance could ruin everything.

My God, this feels so good. With every mouthful he eats I can feel stress leaving my shoulders.

'See! You love this stuff, little man! Nom, nom, nom!'

[Slight cry from son.]

Oh shit, sorry. Stay focused.

He's probably ready for that drink now.

[Grabs his drink from other side of oven.]

'Here we go, mate.' *Wow, he was thirsty.*

Okay, next spoonful.

[Son refuses food and starts screaming again.]

Oh no. I've fucked it. It's Snakes and Ladders, one false move and you're back to the start.

What did that article say? Stay calm? How the fuck are you supposed to stay calm when the person you love most in the world hasn't eaten properly for five days?

PLEASE eat some more, son. For Daddy? In fact, for yourself. You NEED food to survive, mate. Please?

[Tries to jam spoon in son's mouth again.]

How can you go off food in the middle of a meal? He loved this 15 seconds ago and now it's offensive to his tastebuds. He's fussier than that princess with the pea.

And now he's eating the tablecloth. Great. The food I spent half an hour making for him is foul but the £3 tablecloth from Wilko is strangely delicious.

I wish I was this honest in restaurants. Next time food comes over and I don't fancy it, instead of being terribly British and suffering quietly I'm gonna lash my drink at the wall, throw my body backwards and scream like someone's hacking my arm off.

Ah, fuck it. Might as well eat this myself. No wonder I'm getting fat.

[Tucks into food while sobbing.]

How to Act Hard in a Soft Play Centre

Until my boys were born I was only vaguely aware of soft play centres. As I write this I've been to every one within a 50-mile radius of our house.

The centres themselves are deceptively huge, with different sections for different age groups. In some these are strictly policed. At others the staff adopt a much more laissez-faire attitude and it's a goddamn free-for-all. If I had to describe soft play centres in a few words I would go for 'the Wild West with padding'. If you're really unlucky there'll be a birthday party booked in while you're there. I learned the hard way that they are no place to visit with a hangover.

Every time we go to one I feel like I'm walking into battle with a swarm of demented wasps, intent on gashing my eardrums and booting me in the shins. One particular tour of duty was no different, when the boys were 14 months old and we decided to try out a brand-new centre in a very well-to-do neighbourhood. The age zones were all themed on famous cities around the world – all very safe and secure and quite impressive. There was Sydney, with the harbour bridge and opera house; Venice, complete with gondolas and ornate architecture; but unfortunately no sign of Milton Keynes with its roundabouts and heavy traffic.

We paid at the front desk. The lady said that our ticket was only valid for an hour but not to worry as 'It'll feel like longer.'

Within four minutes of arriving I'd been assaulted by a three-year-old. We were just settling into the Manhattan area for the under-threes (skyscrapers and yellow taxis to jump on) and this kid who'd clearly just signed a sponsorship deal with Red Bull came zipping over to us, grabbed one of the balls in the ball pool and launched it straight at my tired, over-caffeinated and under-prepared face. His arm was less than a foot away from me as he released the ball so it point-blank twatted me in the eye. It seemed that even in adulthood I'm still the kid getting pushed around in the playground. Yay me.

It bounced off my eye socket and the little turd ran off, no doubt looking for his next victim. I looked to his dad for some kind of reaction, like a footballer who's been tripped in the box looking to the referee. But his dad showed no concern for the fact that his son had just committed a felony. He just slowly mooched over to him with as much urgency as Shaft on his way to return a library book and said, 'Don't do that, son,' in the most monotone voice since the last Pet Shop Boys album.

CONTROL YOUR KID YOU MASSIVE BELLEND is what I didn't say.

Instead I silently wished haemorrhoids on this man, as our boys continued to crawl round this mini New York area, jaywalking whenever they could.

Just as I was starting to calm down from the previous onslaught, a bunch of kids who were clearly breaching the under-threes-only regulation of Manhattan busted into our little play zone. When you first start taking your baby to the soft play centre, you begin to view older kids in the younger section on a par with war criminals. One lad looked like he was at least nine, if not older, but in order to cleverly cheat the system he was crawling. He was nearly as tall as me (and slightly more masculine) so the whole thing looked ridiculous. I did wonder for a minute if maybe he was just a really young dad, but then I saw him pick his nose and eat the contents which convinced me otherwise.

At this point I was just trying to protect my little boys from these older kids who were now rampaging around the under-three area like Genghis Khan and his seven armies. One kid would stomp past us as another jumped over us. Two would weave among us as objects were launched vaguely in our direction.

In the end I couldn't take any more. Enough was enough.

I stood up. Like a MAN.

And quietly walked over to the girl who was working on the door to snitch on them. I mean, she was paid to deal with this sort of thing, right?

As the hordes of overage revellers were led away from the under-threes area, like a true grass I couldn't make eye contact with any of them. At least not until the last boy was leaving – the overage crawler.

As he tied his jumper around his waist he shot me a look that seemed to say *If this was prison, you'd be watching your back, snitch.*

Luckily for me and my family it wasn't prison. It was a middle-class soft play centre, so we finished our play and went for a very nice lunch.

I was getting bored of going to the same soft play centres all the time but I didn't want the boys to miss out on something just because I wanted an easy life (I use the term 'easy' quite liberally, obvs).

I'd heard about a child-friendly café from our friends Karen and Dom, so I decided to try it out one Monday while Rachel was at work.

We pushed our way through the extra-wide, pram-friendly front door, then shuffled through the internal gate. Short of having a metal detector and internal cavity search, this place made Fort Knox look like a gingerbread house. There was no chance any toddlers were escaping from this gaff – I'm an adult with a 2:1 in English literature and I could barely get in. I've been to open prisons that have less security.

The café consisted of tables and chairs in a horseshoe formation with a large play area in the middle. However, the tables and chairs had lots of sharp corners, and I instantly regretted not going to a safe and squidgy soft play centre like any other Monday.

There were no highchairs left so I put the twins on a small chair each next to a table and jogged over to the bar. It's always tempting to not actually order any food or drink at these places, as with offspring in tow it's completely impossible to consume anything. But British manners kicked in so I ordered a large latte and some toast for the boys. As parents we always complain about our hot drinks going cold before we get a chance to enjoy them but, as though I was a real-life Goldilocks, this coffee was hot enough to burn the actual bollocks off my tongue. (Not that I have 'actual' bollocks on my tongue, you understand. This book would have a different tone and, indeed, title if that were the case. And I doubt you'd currently be sitting on the bus reading a book called *The Man with Bollocks on his Tongue*. Nor have I had anyone else's bollocks on my tongue either. I have nothing against anyone who enjoys the practice, but I firmly hope to reach death without ever having experienced any form of bollocks on my tongue.)

As I carefully walked back to our table, trying not to spill my magma-hot beverage, Ben spotted a door and made a beeline for it. He'd become obsessed with doors lately, and would chase towards them like a dog with a postman. This door happened to be for the ladies' toilets.

As a dad you must keep your male children away from the ladies' toilet door the same way you keep a white pool ball away from the pocket. If they get in there you've got to choose between hoping they emerge without wearing various sanitary products as jewellery, or you make the bold and potentially embarrassing decision to dive in and rescue them.

I get my coffee to our table and just manage to grab Ben by the ankles before he passes the state line into Toiletsville. I put him in the middle of the play area and then I chase Zac around the side of a Wendy house, aware that Ben is happily climbing on a small chair. He's not sitting on it normally because that's simply not the way a toddler operates.

No, in order to master the chair, first you must become the chair.

As I'm chasing Zac, out of the corner of my eye I notice Ben being approached by two little girls. My first instinct is *Well done, son. He'll be fighting them off with a stick soon.*

Then I notice that these two little girls aren't remotely

interested in Ben. They just want the chair he's buggering about on. And they're not in a bargaining mood. They're like a pair of fucking bailiffs.

One grabs the chair legs and the other pushes Ben off. He lands on his head before his body crashes to the ground. You can tell when a toddler is really hurt because the time that elapses between injury and first scream is longer. His mouth opens wider than one of those snakes that eats cats but no sound comes out for what seems like forever. It's that long I even start to wonder if my latte might now be drinkable.

When he finally lets out his scream it sounds like an air-raid siren, giving me a mild version of that tinnitus deafness they use on films when a bomb explodes and the lead character can't hear properly.

For the first time in my adult life I find myself telling off someone else's kids.

The girls are skipping away with the chair, like a pair of four-year-old hoodlums.

I want to shout *YOU FUCKING WITCHES* at the top of my lungs but instead I opt for the much more diplomatic, 'Girls, you've got to be careful.'

One of them turns around to me and says, 'But WE were playing with it before.'

Oh, well that's fine then. Sorry, girls, I didn't realise. Tell you what, next time someone sits in a seat I once perched on in the local park, I'll just set them on fire shall I?

Obviously I didn't say this. I didn't even think it back then.

What I thought (and said) was, 'Well, he's only 18 months old and he's really hurt himself.'

They shrugged their shoulders and looked bored, like when someone starts telling you about a dream they had.

I looked around for their parents but couldn't see anyone. *Probably freebasing cocaine and sucking off strangers for cash round the back,* I thought. *Or even worse, staring at their phones.*

I held Ben in my arms and he started to calm down a bit. Zac had heard all the commotion and had waddled back over. He was pulling at my trouser leg like the world's worst wingman.

Maybe I've watched too many Hollywood blockbusters but my first thoughts were how this would be the first scene of a revenge movie. Next would come a training montage showing Ben learning to walk properly, then run, then hitting the gym and learning jiu-jitsu, before returning to the same café six months later and confronting the girls with a cheesy line.

'Have a seat, ladies!'

Before smashing his own seat over their heads.

I was disproportionately angry. They were just little girls finding their way in the world and they hadn't meant to cause any harm. But they'd hurt my little lad and this was a whole new sensation to try to deal with. I'd always wanted to protect my boys, but that was just a concept until now. We'd had the issues in hospital to begin with, but I was such a novice at that point and they were newborn so I was pretty passive in that period. This was the first time I'd had to protect them from other people. Little girls, in fact. And I'd failed.

It was time to go home.

I took a sip of my latte. And burnt the actual bollocks off my tongue. It seemed to have actually increased in temperature and took several layers of skin off my lips.

The Favourite Teddy

Every child has a favourite teddy. That one little bundle of wool they just can't live without. People write poetry about their first love, but that's normally a fleeting experience that ultimately breaks your heart. Your first teddy stays with you forever.

For the discerning toddler-about-town, a good sleeping teddy cannot simply be purchased from a shop. It has to tick several important boxes.

Firstly, the appearance. It needs to have some serious miles on the clock. Take a look at a brand-new teddy. Now, imagine that box-fresh, innocent bear has been squatting in a crack den for seven months straight and you're getting close to how it *should* look. Ideally it'll also be covered in stains of all shapes and sizes from the three major sources – gob, bladder and backside. These must be of assorted vintage – some still damp and others matured to a pleasant crust. The scent should evoke a peculiar combination of revulsion yet comfort. Lastly, it ABSOLUTELY MUST have an appendage of some kind that can be jammed into one's nose (I cannot stress the last part enough).

Of course, their favourite bear doesn't just appear in this state. It matures over time, only gaining the mantle of Favourite Teddy as it slowly deteriorates in appearance like an alcoholic ex-reality-TV star.

Rachel and I bought them both monkeys but, as with their clothing preferences, they had slightly different reactions to their new toys. Zac didn't care for his much, but with Ben it was an old-fashioned boy-meets-teddy love story. He took Monkey everywhere with him and would hit the roof if we gently suggested that Monkey might want to stay home while we popped out. We had a few false alarms when we temporarily misplaced Monkey, but he'd always turn up. We joked that he was part homing pigeon and that we should enter him in races.

One night we were back at home after a trip staying with Rachel's mum in the Midlands.

'Goodnight, Zac.'

'Bye-bye, Dadda.'

'Goodnight, Ben.'

'Monkey?'

'Don't worry, son. I'll get Monkey.'

I looked round the boy's room. Nothing. Under the cots? Zilch.

Our house always looks like a search for something is in progress anyway – upturned cushions, coats on the floor. Rather than helping, this makes any investigation for lost property virtually impossible. Feeling like a burglar in my own home, I casually roved around the house hoping to spot Monkey's dishevelled little face. When I found myself back in the bathroom for another quick look behind the toilet it became clear this search was proving as difficult as the annual Haystack and Needle Challenge at the local home for the blind.

Where is that cheeky little monkey?

Moving downstairs I turned over cushions and checked behind the fridge.

'Babe, where's Monkey?' I called to Rachel.

Ben was starting to cry upstairs. I emptied a full basket of washing onto the floor.

Where is that little rascal?

The moment a casual little search for something becomes a frantic, shit-the-bed-where-the-fuck-is-it panic scramble is the exact moment it becomes impossible to find anything. Your brain becomes mashed and you need to talk yourself back from the ledge. I'd misplaced my passport once and the feeling was eerily similar, although back then it only meant I'd miss an expensive holiday. This would mean no sleep for us and potentially the entire street.

I opened all the kitchen cupboards and started pulling the pans out. Then, I started throwing stuff about the house, waving my arms about like Mr Tickle after a bag of whizz.

The boys were both crying upstairs.

WHERE IS THAT STUPID TWATTING THING?

That's when I looked at the bin. Overflowing, disgusting. The only option.

Let's dance, motherfucker.

I shoved my hands in like it was a tombola for tramps.

'Babe.' Rachel was patting my shoulder.

'WHAT?'

'Babe. Slow down.'

'WHAT IS IT? HAVE YOU FOUND HIM?'

'We've left him at my mum's.'

She shoved her iPad in front of my face. Her mum was on Skype, holding the bastard in front of the screen.

'Monkey?'

The way she was holding him by the top of his head whilst wearing a very sombre expression was reminiscent of a kidnapper issuing a ransom demand. I'm sure Liam Neeson's character in *Taken* would have dealt with this better than me. I just fell to the sofa and shouted 'Oh bollocks!' in a high-pitched, somewhat camp voice.

I started putting my shoes on.

'What are you doing?'

'I'm going to get him.'

'It's a 200-mile round trip!'

If this was Hollywood and I was the hero, at that point I would've mumbled, 'Then I'll see you at dawn,' as I slipped on my Ray-Bans and leather jacket to go off into the night.

But neither of those things were true, so I kicked my sensible shoes back off and, having what I considered at the time to be a brainwave, grabbed *Zac's* monkey. Knowing full well that Ben wouldn't buy that this perfect specimen was his soulmate, I opened the front door and dropkicked it into the garden. Ideally, I'd have liked to have tied it to a chair and put a few cigarettes out on its face but then I remembered that this was an innocent teddy and not some tough suspect I was trying to crack.

It still looked impeccable, and now the shit-eating smile on its perfect fluffy face was beginning to irritate me. I was just about to put it on the driveway and reverse over it a few times in the car when Rachel shouted that she'd given Ben part of his favourite jigsaw and that had done the trick.

Deep down, I was a little disappointed that I didn't get to do it. What kind of a monster had I become?

There is one other item of significance that, when lost, causes even more pandemonium: the remote control. It was a Thursday morning when we noticed.

It had gone missing before, loads of times. But this time was different. There was a hectic nature to this search, and once we'd checked all the usual places – under the sofa, behind the curtains, inside the oven – worry arrived quicker than heartburn on Christmas Day.

The longest we'd searched before had been a paltry eight minutes, but we'd heard the horror stories – parents forced to watch the CBeebies test-card on date night, or, worse still, make actual conversation.

Hell on earth.

As I lifted the sofa up six inches so my wife could wave a torch underneath and quite literally shine a light on our frankly lacklustre Hoovering policy, an awful thought dawned on me. *What if we never find it?*

Blind panic kicked in. I jumped over to the TV to see if I could operate it manually. After bashing at the buttons like a pensioner on his grandson's Xbox I managed to turn it off and on again and somehow convince it to initiate a software update. As part of me yearned for the days of four channels and big, obvious buttons, I thought of a place we hadn't looked yet.

'THE FRIDGE!' I shouted, and made my way to the kitchen, losing the rest of my dignity as I slipped on a discarded chunky flap pop-up book.

I flung open the fridge door with all the desperation of a hung-over student looking for leftover pizza. No joy. (Although I did find one Mega Blok and a very confused-looking sock, plus used the opportunity to shove a few slices of cheese into my ever-fattening dad face, hoping it would add clarity to my scattered train of thought.)

Once all the key places had come up blank I put it out to my Facebook page. The comments ranged from helpful to ridiculous, ('Check the cat flap!') but were all welcome.

I went to bed that night dreaming of remote controls. Big ones. Little ones. Retro ones with wires. Chunky universal ones. I woke up in a cold sweat after a nightmare about the old Videoplus+ remote my nan used to own (I blame the cheese slices for that).

The second day was tough but at least we still had CBeebies. Or so I thought. It turned out the software update had rendered the TV completely unusable – unless we could find the remote.

The kids were screaming. The parents were losing control. I could barely hold it together.

As I was casually rooting through next door's bin, I had my eureka moment. I grabbed an old remote from the broken stereo system, offered it to my 19-month-old son and asked him to 'Go and put it with the other one.' He took it and toddled off into the dining room. I followed him at a safe distance, like a tracker hunting his prize deer.

He turned round and saw me following him.

'Show Daddy where the other remote is, son. Please? PLEASE?'

He handed the new remote back to me, blew a raspberry and waddled off, laughing his little head off.

I lay my head on the kitchen floor. I wanted to sob but feared if I started I might never stop. The coolness of the kitchen tiles soothed my head and a calmness washed over me like a gentle tide. My eyes dropped to the floor.

And there it was. Underneath the fridge. Covered in fluff and crumbs. It looked so beautiful.

I didn't instinctively reach out and grab it like I'd fantasised I would. Instead I gazed at its simple elegance. I had found my prey.

Until the next time.

Witness the Sickness

Nobody likes being really ill, but I never used to mind feeling a little bit under the weather. That level of poorly where you can just nip to bed with a bottle of Lucozade and a hot water bottle and enjoy a guilt-free marathon of *The Real Housewives of New York City*.

But as soon as kids arrive in your life, getting ill goes from a mild inconvenience to something filed under 'NO LONGER AN OPTION', along with impromptu beers, arriving on time and owning nice things. You simply have to carry on, protecting and providing for your little ones.

The first time I got a stomach bug after the boys were born, I couldn't stop apologising to Rachel as I ducked out of my parental duties and tried to quarantine myself in the spare room.

'It's fine, honestly,' she barked at me in a tone that indicated it clearly wasn't.

Other parents warned us of the lurgy that our boys would start bringing home once they started in childcare, as if their nursery was as disease-riddled as the festering slums of the Victorian era. True to their warning, within the first few months of sharing air with other kids they had brought home more coughs and colds than you'd find in a Crucible World Snooker Championship audience.

If they're ill, you can't take them to nursery but you still have to pay, which smarts like a kick in the knackers.

What actually hurts even more is when you get the lurgy too and can't even take care of them yourself.

It was a Sunday evening and I had driven the two-and-a-bit hours home from a gig in Hartlepool, feeling more and more ropey as the journey went on. When I got back Rachel was in bed, shivering. I tried to comfort her but even holding a conversation with me made her want to vomit (not that unusual), so I went to make her a hot water bottle. Halfway down the stairs I shat myself. By that I don't mean I was suddenly startled – I literally went to the toilet in my own trousers. I think the more hip amongst us call this phenomenon a 'shart' but the presence of a humorous slang name did nothing to cushion the devastating blow of breaking my nearly-34-year streak of not shitting in my own pants that I'd so proudly held.

Rachel must have heard the whole thing. Me confidently jogging halfway down the stairs. Me letting out a cheeky trump. Me stopping dead. Sudden silence. Unfortunately for my very forgiving wife, the trump bit was nothing new. If anything, since the kids had been born the standards by which we conducted ourselves had plummeted to an all-time low. After all, what's a little bottom burp compared to a full-scale double-bath shite that the boys were so keen on administering?

I stood there on the stairs, my feet on different steps, frowning to myself intently.

'Are you okay?'

'Not reeeeeally,' came my surprisingly upbeat reply.

'What's happened?' Her voice sounded weak.

'I've shat myself.'

I heard giggling coming from our bedroom. At least I'd cheered her up. Every cloud and all that, although I'm not sure a silver lining would have been absorbent. And an absorbent lining would have been useful.

The next morning started in as bad a way possible when I woke myself up by doing it again. I couldn't believe it. It gave me an insight into why the boys were so grumpy first thing when they'd woken up in the same predicament. I was furious.

Privately wondering why The Bangles didn't mention this in their 'Manic Monday' song, I cleaned myself up and tried to gather myself for the day ahead. It was impossible. By the time the boys woke up neither Rachel nor I could move without retching. We had piercing headaches and our backsides were busier than Asda on Black Friday. We acted out our own version of *Game of Thrones*, swapping places on the toilet every few minutes like a wrestling tag team.

First task was to get the boys changed. Both of them had decided to fill their nappies with some of the most disgraceful output since Katie Hopkins' Twitter feed. But having shat myself twice in the previous 12 hours I decided to reserve judgement on this occasion.

You get hardened to changing vile nappies as time wears on, but feeling so nauseous added a whole new dimension to the challenge. Retching and gagging, at one point I had to swallow a bit of my own sick. I tried the age-old trick of boosting morale by singing a happy song, but I just didn't have enough zest in me to do it justice. This resulted in the most sub-par rendition of 'Old MacDonald Had A Farm' our house has ever witnessed.

I didn't know how we'd make it through the day. I decided to phone my mum. If she could take the boys, even for just the morning, we might get through this.

She took ages to answer and when she did, it turned out she'd come down with the exact same bug.

We were fucked.

We moved every single toy, jigsaw and book into the lounge and shut the door. If we could keep them occupied in the same room as us maybe we could just lie on the sofa all day. The first 90 seconds were glorious – we lay on a sofa each and occasionally opened one eye to check the boys were occupied.

Then something happened.

Historians have often argued about the real cause of the First World War. I can't bring anything to that particular debate, but if you told me that new evidence indicated that it had all kicked off because Archduke Franz Ferdinand tried to put a corner piece from his farmyard jigsaw into the jungle jigsaw that Kaiser Wilhelm II was in the middle of, I'd totally believe you.

They screamed and scratched and I tried to step in but had to swerve to be sick into my hand. Thankfully the noise of my retching seemed to confuse them and they went back to their own jigsaws.

We spent the rest of the day mainly keeping them away from plug sockets and each other. Now and again I'd throw a new jigsaw into the mix like a zookeeper feeding the lions. Time moved slower than a snail with a gammy foot, and when their bedtime arrived we felt like we'd scaled Everest. I learned that day that it's possible to spend the entire day inside, lying on the sofa, having shat yourself twice, yet still feel immensely proud of your achievements. After surviving the day from hell it appeared that anything was now possible.

A Bad (Restaurant) Trip

I'd always considered myself working-class, until one day I found myself loudly proclaiming, 'Benjamin, you've got moussaka in your hair, sweetheart,' and it was time to face facts.

I had become middle-class.

Before the kids, Rachel and I always enjoyed eating out. We weren't proper foodies but we loved some nice food with a bottle of wine, and at least once a week we'd go out for a few drinks and a meal. Once the boys arrived our social life came to such an emergency stop that I could feel my nose on the dashboard. We were keen to drip-feed this pastime back into our lives but we knew it would be tricky. We'd been out for breakfast a couple of times when the boys were a few months old. That was a piece of piss – they'd sleep right through the hour or so we spent devouring a full English and necking multiple coffees. But taking toddlers to a public eatery has the potential to be as relaxing as having root canal surgery administered by a blind back-street dentist with a twitch. Even if they're behaving themselves, it's only a matter of time before boredom or curiosity gets the better of them and they start throwing stuff on the floor or yelling.

I used to look at parents of toddlers in restaurants and think, *What are you doing here? You're having a terrible time, you can't eat your own food, and your child is ruining the atmosphere for us normal people.* I was about to cross that particular threshold.

It had been a long week. The boys were 19 months old and hadn't been sleeping or eating well, but the gradual erosion of our sanity led us to decide to all go out for our dinner.

'It'll be lovely,' Rachel said in one octave too high to be convincing.

We arrived at the restaurant, a friendly Mexican bar and grill not far from our house, and the place was packed. Northern Soul music was playing as punters sipped drinks at the bar and waiters busily zipped from table to table. We made our way to the maître d'.

'There'll be a 10-minute wait for a table. Is that okay?'

This was our first chance to pull the cord and get the fuck out of there. But we didn't.

'That's fine,' I nodded as we stood in the busy bar area, the boys having already lost what little patience they arrived with. They were properly walking by this point. Before babies learn to walk unaided, they serve their apprenticeship on the edge of the sofa, using it to prop them up. This process is affectionately known as 'cruising' which always made me imagine my two lads driving around in a convertible sports car like *Miami Vice*, trying to pick up chicks and keep the neighbourhood safe.

After missing the first roll, I wasn't taking any chances on missing either of the boys' first steps. This meant that as they got closer to it I was scared to even leave the room. One Sunday afternoon as the boys were 'cruising' round the edge of the sofa, I was busting for a wee so asked Rachel if she'd hold onto them while I nipped to the loo.

'Hold onto them?' she asked.

'Yeah, just stop them from walking for a minute.'

'I'm not stunting our children's development just because you've necked too much coffee.'

I sprinted upstairs to the bathroom and just as I was in full flow Rachel started yelling, 'YES! YES! GO ON, BENNY!'

If you've got kids, you'll know how difficult it is to stop a piss in mid-flow but I didn't want to miss this so I somehow managed it, legged it downstairs while zipping up just in time to see Ben striding across the living room before collapsing in a heap on the floor. Zac joined him a week or so later and then they were walking and falling all over the place, often screaming their heads off before clambering up for another attempt.

Now I was wishing we could rewind to when they'd been immobile. Ben wanted to go off exploring this new forest of legs he was stood in. Zac was intent on reaching a rogue bread roll he'd spotted on the floor. Neither of them wanted to stand still like the law-abiding citizens we hoped they'd become. Rachel was searching for signal on her phone so she could show them something from CBeebies but was having no joy.

I tried to hold both lads on my lap to sing them a song, all the while staring at the maître d', trying to put a Jedi mind trick on him so he'd seat us quicker. But neither twin wanted to sit still and be sung to – they were in a foreign land and wanted to explore that land in depth, until they fell over or were given a fish finger. Whichever came first.

Ten minutes came and went and we still hadn't been seated.

This was our second opportunity to abort the mission and get back to Base Camp. We didn't take it.

Instead we forged ahead, into the great unknown. I'd like to say we were akin to intrepid travellers like Christopher Columbus or Sir Francis Drake, but we were more like a pair of confused pensioners who'd got lost on the way to the 24-hour garage.

After what felt like longer than a 1970s prog-rock drum solo, we were shown to our seats. The boys were in high-chairs and Rachel and I sat opposite each other, monitoring a twin each. I used to love taking an age to decide what to order in restaurants, but not anymore – I chose for everyone as the boys started crying that they wanted to return to the leg forest. After finally managing to make eye contact with the waitress with all the serenity of a man drowning in sulphuric acid, we ordered our food.

The food didn't take ages but by the time it arrived it felt like we'd survived a long, cold winter. We'd forgotten to bring any distractions for the boys (rookie error!) so they were keen on throwing whatever they could reach on the floor.

We both kept remarking how nice it was to be out and what a lovely time we were having, despite clearly hating every second. Our eyes told the real story. We were both eating far quicker than you should in a restaurant (Chinese buffet excepted) so we could get the bill and get out of there. Zac had discovered he could now dribble at will and was conducting an experiment to see how much saliva he could fit on the table. Ben had started blowing aggressive raspberries at all and sundry. People were staring, some of them disapprovingly. As much as you tell yourself it doesn't matter, it definitely detracts from your enjoyment of the evening. I don't care who you are, when you can feel the unfavourable glances from fellow diners digging into you, it's hard to enjoy your enchiladas. And just as I thought I was at breaking point, something incredible happened.

Ben was flicking salsa across the table while Zac was yelling his favourite new noise (a cross between a cough and a scream), when the doors swung open and my favourite family in the world arrived. They'd booked a table so were seated instantly on the opposite side of the restaurant – a mum, dad and a little girl who looked about two. This kid was going fucking mental. Spitting, shouting, punching people. It was like Godzilla had wandered in wearing a nappy. Our boys looked at her and then at us as if to say, *We're not that bad, are we?*

If this kid had turned up at a restaurant I was in before kids I would have been appalled. On this occasion, I looked at her like she was a superhero.

Whilst speed-eating my chicken burrito that night I learned that in a parents' dictionary the definition of relief is 'When a noisier child than your own turns up at the restaurant.'

It's Like Pulling Teeth

At 18 months, Rachel and I received a letter saying we should take the boys to the dentist. The letter, from our local surgery, said it was more to get them used to the environment – sitting in the chair, getting the light shone on you, stuff like that. I argued that if we really wanted to give them a genuine British dental experience we should read to them from a four-year-old copy of *Take a Break*, ask the receptionist to be rude, and then charge them £35.60 for naff-all.

We arrived early.

I know this is printed so you could easily just go back to the previous line and check you read it correctly but I'm going to say it again.

WE ARRIVED EARLY.

And let me say this – it felt weird. We hadn't been early for anything since (ironically) the boys arrived a month early into the world, kicking and screaming. So used as we were to rushing and racing to get out the house and get where we were going, this was all so relaxed.

Your attitude to time keeping relaxes so much as a new parent. Those who previously ran regimes stricter than North Korea often shift to something approaching 1970s San Francisco. With kids, if you arrive within 45 minutes of the agreed time, you're not *technically* late. I'm not sure this has been agreed on legally but I'm buggered if I'm apologising for being a wee bit tardy when I've had four hours broken sleep and my kids have decided to hide my car keys in the back of the salad drawer of the fridge. There's also the fact that at this point it's unlikely you're meeting anyone without kids themselves. If you are, and they're late, it's probably because they overslept. So they deserve zero sympathy.

(I've also discovered that with your kids in tow, even if you feel like you're on schedule, the correct term is 'not late yet'. Anything could happen to delay your arrival – someone could lose a shoe, there could be a major wobbler thrown because you cut the toast the 'wrong' way – anything at all.)

But on this occasion, nothing got in the way. Everything went smoothly. It was eerie.

We arrived at the dentist a full 10 minutes before their appointments. And as soon as we walked into the waiting room, we lost control. Both pipsqueaks wrestled free and started running around like they'd just escaped a prison van. It was like an early Prodigy gig, if the Prodigy were two foot tall and wearing nappies.

We herded them into the corner, like a pair of bedraggled sheep dogs who've lost most of their flock and all of their touch. There was an old activity table with the same old rubbish that's always in waiting rooms – building blocks and an old wooden abacus that looked like it'd seen more action than Andy McNab. (I've yet to see a child actively enjoy an abacus. I understand that they represent numbers and maths – I get that part. But they're boring and often covered in slobber. I bet even the friends of the person who invented the abacus thought it was rubbish.)

Then Ben spotted the stairs and he might as well have been a Labrador that knows it's time for his walk – he was desperate to get up them.

Rachel and I were in possession of a twin each, but a massive hatchet was thrown into the works as the receptionist called us over to fill in all the relevant forms for the boys' first visit. In this environment, a little bit of admin seemed very attractive, and we both tried to grab the pen from her like a pair of piss-poor relay runners.

Rachel won the tussle for the pen, during which, Ben, completely unmonitored by either of us, was already halfway up the bloody stairs. Seizing him and putting him back near the abacus, I noticed that Zac had obviously decided that the dentist wasn't for him and was trying to open the front door that led out onto the busy main road.

I speed-walked over to him and dragged him back to the abacus too.

But Ben was halfway up the stairs again, so I pulled him back down, trying to keep the mood light.

And now Zac was back at the front door, stood on tiptoes trying to get purchase on the handle.

Fighting the urge to scream I was desperate to somehow demonstrate to the room of complete strangers that I was in control, despite being anything but. I moved Zac back to the abacus and nipped over to Rachel to ask her to hurry up but she just smiled at me and got back to her forms.

Zac was now back at the front door so I picked him up again and tried to distract him with the abacus but he wasn't interested. I did a quick parental scan of the room once – and couldn't see Ben. Nausea enveloped me. I shouted his name, then again. The third time my voice was almost cracking with the tension.

'WHERE'S BEN?'

Rachel pointed towards my shoes. He was standing underneath me, tugging at my trousers. He'd been there the whole time. Relief flooded my body, with an embarrassment chaser.

We spent less than two full minutes inside the dentist's room and he said he thought the boys adjusted to the situation pretty well.

I was glad to hear that because I knew that I certainly hadn't.

No Sex Please, We're Parents

Rachel and I had our first night away without the kids when they were 20 months old. Hotel, dinner and a few drinks. We'd also pencilled in a bit of 'mummy and daddy time' if you catch my drift. If you don't know what I'm talking about then you must be getting less of it than me. Nowadays we have to schedule in sex with at least three full working days' notice and a complete veto allowed at any time from either party.

We spent the entire morning kissing the boys goodbye. I felt excited but sad, like when you find yourself in McDonald's for the second day on the trot. I'm sure they wanted to say, *You two go on and have fun. You deserve it after all you've done for us*. But one blew a raspberry and the other chewed at the sock that was still on his foot. They clearly gave a grand total of zero shits about us leaving.

We made a list longer than the Yellow Pages for the grandparents – what to do, how and when to do it. How much to use, which way to wipe and where to put it afterwards. Then we loaded up the car – in five minutes. FIVE MINUTES! At this stage, if leaving the house goes from concept to reality in less than an hour then you've definitely forgotten something. Maybe one of the kids.

We waved to the boys and they ignored us. To be fair, one looked like he was trying to squeeze a poo out. As we drove off into the sunset, we both felt weird. We glanced at each other with a nervous smile, like we were doing something wrong. Something illegal. We remarked how it felt like we'd DEFINITELY forgotten something, but in truth we both felt empty. Looking in the rear-view mirror and not seeing our two little boys was horrible.

But we knew they'd be okay. They were in safe hands.

Or were they? My parents brought me up well enough but that was years ago and the game has changed since then. Back in the 1980s you could just throw your kids a shard of glass and a coat hanger to play with while you went down the mine for 12 hours. It was a simpler time to now – my dad can't work a mobile phone and my mum initially thought the iPad was a sanitary product.

I was nervous and could feel the sharp edge of panic starting to poke me. By the time we passed the next junction all my worries had been put through the 'worst-case scenario' filter in my mind and I was now imagining scenarios more ludicrous than Donald Trump's inclusion on the cover of *Hairstyle Monthly*.

I called my Dad. 'Hi, Dad. It's me.'

'Oh, hiya, son. What's up?'

'Nothing really, just wanted to check everything was okay?'

'You've only been gone two minutes.'

'A lot can happen in two minutes, Dad.'

'Good point. You were conceived in less.'

'Oh Jesus, Dad. Do you really have to?'

'I did that night, son.'

'For God's sake, Dad. The kids – is everything okay?'

'Yes. Of course it is.'

We checked into the hotel – a spa resort in the middle of the English countryside – and went straight to the room. Our modus operandi was to relax. Turn our brains off for 24 hours, enjoy each other's company and get a good night's sleep after a little bit of you-know-what. I made the mistake of testing the mattress as soon as we got to our room. My wife tried to step in but her flailing arms couldn't quite reach me.

'DON'T LIE DOWN!'

It was too late. My back hit the top of the duvet and everything went into slow motion. My legs bounced down onto the bed runner and I sank like an iPod Nano into a bowl of soup.

It started out as a blink, but then my eyes decided to clock off and not open again, suddenly heavy and stubborn as an old garage door. My head span and the world shut down. Through the fog of sleep whirling around me I could just make out a distant noise.

'Dddddddd . . .'

The feeling was delicious.

'Dddddddd . . .'

I was jolted out of my slumber by my wife grabbing me by the shoulders and yelling in my face: 'Don't you FUCKING DARE fall asleep!'

I felt like I'd been fished out of a coma via CPR. I needed a drink.

We headed down to the bar and ordered lunch and a pint of Guinness each. We weren't planning to drink much but it was nice to have a pint during the day. We polished off our food and ordered another pint of the black stuff.

I was beginning to relax.

As we got ready for dinner it took me back to our old holidays before the kids came along. Of course, back then my pants used to fit. Now even my undies felt tight, and the buttons on my shirt were so taut I feared the waiter might lose an eye if I reached for my wallet.

I was careful not to sit on the bed this time. That beautiful bastard would sucker me in again, I knew it.

At dinner the wine and conversation was flowing as we covered the following topics:

- The kids
- How much we missed the kids
- Trying to figure out what we talked about before the kids

Were they okay? We hadn't had an update for a while. I tested my phone for signal, then texted myself to check I was still receiving. Then I received a text which made me relax until I realised it was the one I'd just sent myself. All fine but no update.

Another 10 minutes went by as I glugged my wine and stared at my phone. This wasn't relaxing in the slightest. I figured by now the boys were probably embarking on a Skittles and Red Bull-fueled rampage, swinging from the light fittings like gremlins. I gave my mum a call.

No answer.

My old friend Panic returned (he'd never really left if truth be told) so I rang the house phone. It got to the seventh ring and I was about to hang up when my mum answered.

'Hello?'

'Mum! It's me! Is everything okay? WHY CAN I HEAR CRYING IN THE BACKGROUND?'

'Because some idiot just rang the house phone and woke everyone up – that's why.'

I'd never considered myself to be an uptight person so this felt like new territory for me. I apologised, she assured me they were okay, and Rachel and I had a celebratory cocktail.

We capped the night off with a whiskey at the bar that I neither wanted nor enjoyed. Make no mistake, we were now shitfaced. Not party drunk either; we were put-me-in-a-taxi-and-don't-worry-I'll-find-my-other-shoe-tomorrow pissed, and ready for bed.

On the way back to the room we half-heartedly talked about the previously scheduled sex with all the enthusiasm of a pair of football fans trudging through the snow just because they had season tickets.

In the end I went for a 'quick poo' that took longer than anticipated, and when I emerged from the bathroom she'd fallen asleep. I lay on that beautiful mattress and passed out, dreaming about my glorious lie-in.

At 6.20 a.m. I jumped up like a soldier who's been conditioned for battle. Realising where we were I went back to sleep until 7 a.m. when the relaxing breakfast in bed arrived an hour early and woke us up by knocking on the door like a fucking bailiff.

We packed our stuff as our heads banged. I felt like shit.

'We need a night away,' I suggested. Rachel laughed. I wasn't joking.

I considered ringing to see if the boys were okay but decided they were probably fine. Much more pressing was how I was going to get through the day with a hangover the size of Cornwall.

In fact, all I could think about on the way home was how we needed to do this again, soon. And that next time I'd be careful not to drink like a single man in his 20s when I'm an exhausted dad of twins in his late 30s.

It Takes Two to Tantrum

I consider myself to be a modern parent, meaning that if my kid slips over in mud there'll be a picture uploaded to Instagram way before I've picked him up.

Parenting in the modern age has changed dramatically. Technological developments and environmental changes have played a part but gender roles in Western society have also evolved dramatically. Seeing dads on their own with their kids isn't unusual anymore, whereas I don't remember my dad taking me and my younger brother out on his own, ever.

I go out with the boys on my own whenever I can, and like most parents I've become more comfortable with every incident-free trip we've had. But one particular trip out was different. I'd never had to deal with anything like this before.

I'd forgotten to buy nappies. We only had two left and the boys were shitting with all the regularity of a pair of cuckoo clocks. One of us needed to go and get some and the shops were due to close within the hour. I volunteered, since it was my mistake and I wanted to rectify it.

Rachel protested. 'What, and leave me here with these two bundles of joy?'

It'd been a pretty lousy fortnight. Teething was causing their nappies to be loose and their tempers short. At any given moment, a regional heat for Tantrum of the Year would break out in the house.

'Today was definitely . . .' Rachel paused.

'Challenging?' I offered.

'Bollocks,' she confirmed.

I nodded.

Before kids, nipping to the supermarket on a Saturday evening to grab a few bits while your partner lies on the sofa is quite rightly seen as a bit of a pain in the arse. After your little ones arrive, the mere thought of elbowing your way down the frozen food aisle to get near the BOGOFs feels like a five-star fortnight in Barbados compared with another hellish afternoon of trying to placate an angry, teething toddler who doesn't want to do the jigsaw they've just begged you to get down from the shelf.

ME: 'But you said you wanted to do a jigsaw?'

SON: 'I did. Now I don't. Okay?'

(I've used creative licence here – my son's contribution to this conversation was mainly conveyed via vowels and screaming.)

I couldn't go to the shop on my own – that wasn't fair. And I didn't want to let Rachel win the 'holiday', so I chose to utter the most ill-advised sentence since 1987 BBC weatherman Michael Fish told the nation 'There will not be a hurricane' the day before there was a hurricane.

'I'll take the kids to Asda with me then.'

She looked at me like I'd offered to swim to the moon.

'Are you sure?'

I'm a modern dad, I thought. *I can do these things.*

'It'll be fine, don't you worry.'

'You'll never make it!'

I'd love to say she breathlessly cried this to me in the tone of a damsel in distress as I heroically set off for battle. Instead she snorted it as she closed the front door and left us to begin our suicide mission.

I felt like Roy Scheider in *Jaws*. I'd prove her wrong. I'd prove them all wrong. I was coming back with a fucking shark under my arm.

The boys cried as I put them into their car seats. They complained about the straps being too tight, which made me feel like an arresting officer taking them downtown.

The traffic was heavy and the supermarket car park was packed. I tried the parent and child spaces but as usual they were all taken. I didn't have time to shout at the young guy in a smart car who, judging by the sprightly and optimistic expression on his face was clearly childless. Prick.

I carried on and managed to find a spot.

I couldn't find a trolley with a double seat so considered putting one in the seat and letting the other one trolley-surf his way through the journey. I decided against this, realising that it wasn't safe and would definitely have resulted in an incident.

I didn't really want to leave them in the car unattended but I couldn't see a trolley, so I locked them in and set off to find one. Before too long I'd walked at least 100 yards. Aware that I was on the verge of basically abandoning my kids I went back to the car and got them out.

Dragging the boys alongside me I managed to find a double trolley. It's times like this you really find out who your friends are, and my trolley-token keyring had turned out to be a little turd who'd buggered off at the first sign of trouble.

No bother, I'll just use a pound instead.

Naturally, my last pound coin had been spent on a terrible Peppa Pig ride for the boys earlier that morning. They'd cried as soon as it started moving so the whole thing had been a pointless endeavour.

The mission simply wasn't possible without a trolley. I had cursed this fact several times before, as the nappies were right in the bowels of the store. If I ruled the supermarket world they'd be outside next to the charcoal and flowers. But then if I ruled that world there'd also be snipers on the roof to shoot any misusers of the parent and child spaces, so perhaps I'm not the best person for that job.

We went back to the car and I put them back into their seats. The dream was over before it had even begun. We had no trolley, no money and we had to head home. Broken, broke and nappyless.

That was when I noticed the cash machine. Its neon light was shining through the drizzle, guiding us towards it like the star of Bethlehem. If I could get there and withdraw a tenner, I could buy something little and use the change to grab a trolley. We'd have to walk and cross a busy road but there was a zebra crossing.

I got both boys back out of the car and we set off towards the cash point. As we approached the road I had to carefully adjust my grip – tight enough to prevent any escape attempts but not so tight that they'd be in pain and start kicking off. With one twin on either side of me I felt like

I was skiing. Mainly in the sense that I didn't want to be here and it was getting quite dangerous.

Both lads seemed to be enjoying their little adventure though, and that's when I got a bit cocky.

This is the kind of dad I want to be. I'll take them camping and we'll go to Glastonbury and we'll build rafts and live in a yurt and go travelling and they'll thank me for enriching their lives and broadening their horizons.

As we walked over the zebra crossing I pictured us all on the cover of The Beatles' *Abbey Road*, and that was the moment Ben decided to sit down. On the list of places that are totally inappropriate for a little sit-down I'd say that the middle of a main road has got to make the top three, probably just below an airport runway and any wedding dance floor when 'Don't Stop Me Now' by Queen comes on.

Having no time to begin the delicate negotiation process I scooped him and Zac up and ran to the pavement, wrenching my back in the process. One of the drivers actually beeped and I silently wished him nothing but haemorrhoids.

The cash point was right there but now there was a queue and the rain had got a little heavier.

A homeless gentleman sitting at the side of the cash point was asking everyone for loose change. When he saw me he offered up the now very common 'Ooh, you must have your hands full!'

It felt strange to be offered sympathy by a man with one shoe and no fixed abode. For a minute I was tempted to ask *him* for a quid for the trolley but decided against it.

I got the tenner. Now we had to get back to the shop to get the change.

Near the entrance there was a load of cereal on offer. I shoved a box of Shreddies under my arm and dragged the boys to the 'Nine Items or Less' till. I did have a quick look for the 'Quick Change for a Trolley While Your Toddlers Test Your Patience' till but, despite continual pressure from the public, Asda still hasn't launched these.

As we got to the till, a guy with a basket full of exactly nine items dived in front of us. What a bastard. I should have politely asked if he'd mind us going in front with our one item but my brain was frazzled. And anyway, this is Great Britain, so I just stood there in silence.

Maybe I should sneak an extra item into his basket, I thought. I could then cry foul to the shop assistant and hope to be moved up the queue. I even considered encouraging the boys to do this job for me, like some reverse-Fagin. Of course, I did none of this. I just queued behind him, shaking my Shreddies like they were a huge passive-aggressive maraca.

We bought the Shreddies and got the change.

The boys were starting to get pretty pissed off at this point and it was hard to blame them. Toddlers' moods can often be like the British weather – unpredictable and guaranteed to ruin a picnic.

When your child loses their marbles for no reason, you can slightly detach yourself from it all. Of course you need to respond and keep them safe, but ultimately it's just toddler shit, innit? Part of the parental landscape. When you've caused the tantrum yourself, you're filled with guilt and self-hatred, as well as a fresh bout of tinnitus. If you go camping in the UK you're a fool to not expect rain. And if you drag two toddlers in and back out of Asda before you've even picked up your frigging trolley you can expect an international incident.

It makes me snort when a non-parent friend sees one of my boys get a little bit cross at something and says, 'Uh-oh! Do they have many tantrums?'

I have to stop myself from grabbing their arm with both hands, twisting different ways and shouting, 'WHAT IS THIS?!'

'You're hurting me!'

'TELL ME!'

'It's a Chinese burn, now get off me!'

'THAT'S RIGHT, IT'S A CHINESE BURN. AND A CHINESE BURN IS NOT A NUCLEAR FUCKING ASSAULT, JUST LIKE WHAT YOU SAW JUST NOW IS NOT A TANTRUM. OKAY?'

Sometimes there are warning signs that a tantrum's on its way. Other times it appears quicker than a wasp at a barbecue. It took me a while to understand that there's literally no way to pull them out of the tantrum zone once they're fully immersed. You have to wait for them to leave of their own accord. Until they do, it's pure damage-limitation.

We were just inside the store entrance when Ben pulled the cord and went for it. He lost his footing slightly and embarked on one of those five-second prat-falls that Chaplin himself would've been proud of. Zac went for a different move, instead lowering himself down first onto his bottom, and then slowly arching his back until his entire body was on the floor. It was very graceful, like he was pioneering a new form of angry yoga.

The scorn people fire your way with their eyes when your kid is having a public tantrum is astonishing. You'd probably get a warmer reception from fellow shoppers if you goose-stepped your way round Asda completely bollocko, juggling a pair of steaming fresh jobbies while singing 'Come On Eileen'.

Everyone was now staring at me. As Zac held on to the shelving with both hands with a vice-like grip and Ben did windmills on the floor as I tried to pull his arm, it did actually look like I was trying to kidnap them both. Had I been genuinely trying to swipe them, I definitely would've given up at this point.

We staggered outside and I found a loose double trolley, meaning I didn't actually need the newly acquired pound coin in my hand after all.

BASTARD.

This sent my blood pressure into orbit, which wasn't helped at all by my next task.

Trying to get your child to do anything mid-tantrum is impossible. Attempting to get their legs into a supermarket trolley seat while they thrash, scream and do bicycle kicks should be an Olympic sport. If it had been anything else on my shopping list I would have aborted the mission at that point. Pulled the parachute cord and floated down to safety. But it was nappies. You need them.

I momentarily considered my other options – we could go all hippy-dippy and fashion some cloth ones out of old towels, or call Deliveroo and see if they'd bring some round to our house – but the screeching of Ben pulled my focus back sharply to reality.

I'd managed to wedge both his legs into the same leg hole and he was very unhappy about this. I knew this because he bit me on the arm while pulling my glasses off. I was beginning to worry that we'd be featured on the news if we didn't get the job done soon, so I forced both boys into the trolley and started running down the aisles like I was on a post-apocalyptic *Supermarket Sweep*.

Zac continued to choke on his tears as if they were made of gravel, in that worrying way that toddlers do. Ben kept shouting 'NO!' at the top of his voice, stopping only when he managed to grab a load of Creme Eggs to throw on the floor.

I grabbed three boxes of nappies and on the way out happened to pass the wine and chocolate sections, grabbing shitloads of both in the process.

By the time we got to the till they'd quietened down. When we reached the car they were in quite good spirits. As we drove home I took several deep breaths and sarcastically asked them, 'Did you enjoy that, boys?'

'Yeah,' they both replied. I suppose everyone needs a hobby.

I opened the front door and Rachel was just waking up from a snooze. I was battered and bruised, mentally and physically scarred, but I had survived, and more importantly, I had the nappies.

I had returned with a shark under my arm. Even if that shark has taken a huge bite out of my sanity.

Winston Churchill famously said, 'If you're going through hell, keep going.' I can only assume he was referring to tackling the weekly shop with a pair of demented toddlers.

Dear Dad

I've learned so much over the past two years – mostly about myself. I've discovered that I have far more patience than I thought possible, found out I could survive on three hours' sleep a night, and that I'm quite comfortable wearing ladies' maternity pants.

But what have I actually learned about being a parent? At times it's felt like I've just scratched the surface and that there's so much more to grasp. All the stuff I eventually nailed is now more useless than being able to rap the lyrics to *The Fresh Prince of Bel-Air* theme tune. I can wind a baby (no use to me now), I know how to assemble and collapse the big pram (which we no longer use), and by the time I finally memorised which Teletubby was which, the boys had decided they HATED that show.

That's because parenthood is a crafty bastard. The second you master something it changes the game so you're shit at it again.

I was always a slow learner but it's never really mattered before. This stuff matters. Some days I've felt out of my depth and slightly overwhelmed by the road ahead of me. I still do. There are so many questions and no definitive answers. How will I teach my kids right from wrong? How can I discipline them and retain a healthy relationship? Why the hell won't they eat their pasta? What school should they go to? How do I get their dummies off them? Should they even have dummies? Are they watching too much TV? Can I pick them up when they're crying? Is it okay to shout at them? Whose maternity pants are these?

How do other people get a handle on it?

Over time, and through writing my blog, I've had numerous conversations (both real and online) with parents far more experienced than me. It soon became clear that many of them felt the same way as me, even when their kids were much older and, in some cases, had moved out and even become parents themselves. That's when I started to realise – *you can't learn this completely.*

It's impossible to do so. The goalposts are always shifting, the rules always changing. Your kids are growing, you're growing. Everything is in flux and it will be until it's time to put on your big coat and make the long walk over to the next life.

Life is full of moments – everyone's life is. But when your kids are born, especially when they're small, those moments swarm around you.

Sometimes it's a landmark – taking their first steps or saying their first word. Other times it's just a smile, a glance or an unexpected hug, and for that one short moment the entire world makes sense. And when your child laughs, the world *really* makes sense (unless they're laughing at the bollocking you've just given them, in which case you might need to review your approach to discipline). These are the moments that I've learned to store away in my memory, as they provide solace when the next parental challenge arises.

I can't ever foresee a time when I won't be a Learner Parent, even when I'm helping my kids move out or welcoming my first grandchild into the world. (Learner Grandparent, anyone?)

But ultimately – when you're there in the eye of the storm – it's difficult to assess your own progress, so I think it's only fair that my boys themselves have the last word.

Thanks for reading and I hope you've enjoyed my book.

Dear Dad,

It's been a rollercoaster two years, and on the whole you've done a decent job. You've given us food and stopped us licking the plug sockets, and for that we thank you.

However, we think you'd admit yourself that a few things have been desperately below par. We hope you don't mind, but in an attempt to bring some form of order to our lives – heaven knows there's none of that at the moment – we've put them into a short list.

SINGING
We appreciate the motives behind your relentlessly hideous upbeat warbling but you MUST increase your repertoire. 'The Wheels on the Bus'? Please. That was grating before our first tooth. These days we'd rather sleep in a puddle of our own

hot piss than listen to your cheap crooning. You sound like a tone-deaf yak copulating with an alarm clock.

Also - FYI - dinosaurs don't ride the bus. Have you been smoking weed?

And don't get us started on Old MacDonald. We don't give a flying fuck about his farm and nor should you. Get your own house in order before you start worrying about anyone else's. You're like a two-hit wonder with that shit. Have you ever been to see a band and they sing their one famous song early on and you just KNOW they're gonna play it again before they finish? Well, that.

NAPPY CHANGES

You were godawful at the beginning. Fuck me, it was embarrassing to even be involved. We used to lie there thinking, This bellend's forgotten the wipes again! Who even does that?

Remember when you did everything perfectly but then forgot to put a new nappy on? Of course you do because you did it again the following day. We used to think we'd be better doing it ourselves.

In fairness, you have improved. Vastly. But we've changed too. We're not going to lie still anymore - we're going to roll, kick, stab, gouge, grab, throw and shit on your arm whenever we can. So please, keep up. And you probably need to think about potty training soon, so good luck with that because we can't wait.

FEEDING

Some days we like chicken, some days we don't. Some days we like beef, today we preferred our shoes. Tomorrow we might fancy a bit of fried rubber with a side order of fuck-all - who knows? We can't help it if our tastebuds are all messed up. It's Mother Nature, man.

It's probably not a great idea to come at us with those monster portions either. Have you seen the size of us? We're TINY. When you throw down a plate of food that's bigger than our heads, of course we're gonna scream.

Mealtimes shouldn't be a challenge. This isn't Man v. Food. It's Father v. Sons, and we all know who's winning. So give us what we want and make sure it's ice cream.

(Also, you get very annoyed when we throw food off the table, but don't take it personally. We just love that sound it makes as it splatters across the kitchen floor. Glorious!)

TEACHING US TO TALK

Okay, so we haven't started talking properly yet. And yes, other kids have. And do you know what? We don't give a shit. Stop stressing, we'll get there when we're ready.

Those early talkers at nursery have got no personality anyway.

NAPPING

Sometimes we simply do not need or want to sleep. Deal with it. Just because we're screaming, rubbing our eyes and yawning doesn't mean we're tired. Most of the time we're just fuming that, yet again, you've taken us away from playtime. There's so much entertainment to be had, and when you incarcerate us in our cots we're missing out. That mirror in the hallway? Incredible. Slapping the window sill? Priceless. Interrupting you on the toilet? NEVER GETS OLD!

By the time we get to your decrepit age we'll probably also be jaded by experience and weakened by overexposure to the world. But you must understand, this place is the most insane party since we left those disgusting loins of yours.

Anyway, why don't YOU get more sleep if it's so important?

SO LET'S DO A QUICK RECAP, SHALL WE?

We're learning a new language, eating food we don't like, figuring out how to talk, our teeth are killing us, and if we need a poo we just have to go in our pants. IS IT ANY SURPRISE WE GET A BIT FUCKED OFF SOMETIMES?

If you had to learn to juggle while talking Portuguese and pissing yourself, I reckon you'd get a bit eggy too.

But aside from that, you're a decent fella and we're genuinely fond of you. Sometimes you have no clue what you're doing, but that's alright because we don't know what you should be doing either. We're all learning here. So hang in there, because whatever you get wrong we're still going to love you. (Except when we become teenagers, obvs. Then we'll probably hate you for a bit.)

Lots of love,

Ben and Zac xx

P.S. Keep up the good work with Peekaboo. We don't know where or how you came up with it but God bless you, it's tremendous. We'll never grow tired of that.

Acknowledgements

In my wildest dreams I never thought that what started off as a simple way of remembering key moments with my kids would evolve into an actual book! It really is a dream come true and I'm incredibly thankful to so many people so I'll try not to miss anyone out. Here goes:

Nothing I've done in life would have been possible without the unwavering love, support and friendship of my mum and dad. If I can replicate half of that with my boys then I'll be so happy. And to Alex, Vicki and little Louie for being the best brother, sister-in-law and nephew I could hope for.

This book wouldn't have been made without the lovely people who've read, shared and commented on my blog over the last couple of years so a MAHOOSIVE thanks to all of you! Often you're much funnier than me.

Huge thanks to Amanda, Anna, Mark and all the team at Seven Dials for showing faith in me while being supportive and constructive. And to my brilliant editor Emily Barrett – I never used to understand why authors thanked their editor but BOY do I understand now. Thanks for shaping my ramblings into something much more coherent. To Juliet at

Caskie Mushens – thanks for being a super agent (in both senses) and for explaining what industry terms mean in a way that my simple head can understand!

To all of the incredible staff at the Women's Hospital and Alder Hey who brought my boys into the world and took care of them when they were fragile and poorly, I will never stop thanking you as long as I live. And to all the families I met at Alder Hey who weren't as lucky as us – your strength continues to be an inspiration.

To Ste, Leila and all of the Coogans – you helped us in ways you'll never know by being there just when we needed you. Thank you.

To all of the people I lived with and met through the Flat 6 years in Haigh Court – thanks for bringing me out of my shell and making me realise that I could actually make strangers laugh – that changed everything.

To my musical brothers in dBh, maybe one day I'll write about that?! And to the other Two Amigos – thanks buddies.

Thanks to Lynne Gerrard and Mike Lindley for encouraging me to start my blog in the first place and explaining to this luddite how the whole thing works. And to the other bloggers and websites who shared their kind words or featured me early on: Netmums, Tamba, Elephant Journal, The Unmumsy Mum, When Skies Are Grey.

Thanks to Gillian Miller and everyone at The Comedy Trust for keeping me busy and to Iain Christie at the Royal Court Theatre for helping me with some of the chapter titles. And to Gav Cross for his patience in helping me set up my podcast.

Finally, to my wonderful wife Rachel for her never-ending love and support. And to my beautiful boys, Zac and Ben. I could write a book a hundred times this size about the happiness, joy and love you've brought into my life. Thank you.

About the Author

Sam Avery, a quasi rock star in his 'youth' and a stand-up comedian ever since, started a blog when his twin boys were born to share his parenting jubilations and tribulations. Within months he had won Best New Blog at the MAD awards and saw the devoted following to his Facebook page, which he updates regularly, skyrocket. He has been featured in the *MailOnline*, the Lad Bible, Netmums and the *Liverpool Echo* and makes regular appearances on 5 Live and BBC Radio 6 Music. You can find regular posts on his Facebook page, @samaverylearnerparent; download a new episode of, 'The Learner Parent Podcast' every Friday on iTunes; and see what he's up to on his Instagram, @thelearnerparent.